Identifying Small Habits

Identifying Small Habits

Left Unchecked by School Leaders, Small Faults Can Become Major Cracks

Larry Dake

ROWMAN & LITTLEFIELD
Lanham • Boulder • New York • London

Published by Rowman & Littlefield
An imprint of The Rowman & Littlefield Publishing Group, Inc.
4501 Forbes Boulevard, Suite 200, Lanham, Maryland 20706
www.rowman.com

86-90 Paul Street, London EC2A 4NE, United Kingdom

British Library Cataloguing in Publication Information Available

Library of Congress Cataloging-in-Publication Data

*This book is dedicated to those who have pushed me to achieve beyond
what I thought was possible at the time. In particular, I dedicate this book
to Mr. Howard Fedrick, King's College (PA) history professor for more than
twenty years until his death in 2011. Mr. Fedrick pushed a less-than-serious
18-year-old freshman to expect excellence in all endeavors—a flame
that was lit and will hopefully never be extinguished. Mr. Fedrick taught
me that if I dedicated myself to a task, the outcome could be great.*

Contents

Preface

This book was written for school leaders who already demonstrate effectiveness in their practice, and possess potential to achieve even greater results. All leaders, regardless of their demonstrated outcomes, have room to grow and often those areas of growth are found in addressing small habits that hinder greater growth. While my first book, *Crisis Management: Effective Leadership to Avoid Early Burnout* was designed for prospective and early career leaders, this book is intended for a wider audience.

All leaders possess blind spots in their practice that, over time, can hinder effectiveness. In addition, many leaders fall into routines and habits around ineffective practices. Some of these practices, such as relying on email too frequently as a communication tool, are seemingly small. Over time, however, engaging in too many of these bad leadership habits can have a detrimental effect on a building or organization's culture, climate, and student outcomes. Being intentional about identifying these habits, surfacing the practices, and addressing them before they widen into deep fissures is crucial.

Out of this approach, *Identifying Small Habits* was written. This book surfaces thirty-eight leadership habits that often fly under the radar and may not be noticeable to leaders at first. While others may take note of these practices, leaders themselves often fail to see their impact because they are baked-into their daily routines. Each of these habits, by itself in small doses, may not be detrimental to leadership effectiveness. However, practiced over time through established patterns and routines, they have the potential to negatively impact a leader's work and their building and organization's goals.

Reflecting upon these habits and correcting them before they negatively impact culture, climate, and outcome is essential. Each chapter reviews one such seemingly small, yet impactful habit and unpacks why it necessitates identification and improvement. Then, chapters delve into strategies to turn such bad habits around. It is not enough to identify such a habit in our leadership practice; we must also know what steps to take to ameliorate its negative impact and contribute to our leadership growth.

As aforementioned, this book is organized into thirty-eight small chapters, each identifying and strategizing around one small habit. It is designed to be a book that the reader can read cover to cover, or jump around to chapters that pique their interest. Each chapter is easily digestible and concludes with either a reflective question or thought around leadership practice. It is intended to be a book about practical leadership thinking rather than one that explores leadership research and theory.

This book's brainchild stems from my own leadership practices over the last dozen years as well as my work with new and veteran school leaders. In my role as an educational leadership program adjunct professor, I have worked with nearly 75 prospective school leaders coming through our program and remained in touch with most of them as they attain their initial and subsequent administrative positions. While educational leadership programs lead to certification and qualifications, they often do not teach the little things that make or break leadership, especially in those early years.

For example, understanding the school budget from beginning to end—and all the nuances in between—is an important knowledge base. The reality, however, is that most school leaders are not responsible for their district's overall budget. That responsibility usually rests with the Superintendent or someone else in a district-level leadership position. The early career Assistant Principal or five-year leader who just attained their first Principalship is likely not responsible for all aspects of school funding.

Rather, what makes or breaks those leaders are often smaller, more mundane practices. Being open to feedback, being visible in the building, and practicing effective communication habits is more important for these leader's success than understanding how a state's tax levy system works. For these leaders, this book will address those smaller, more mundane habits and unpack how they can make or break leadership effectiveness, career paths, and a building or organization's overall outcomes.

Moreover, established and effective school leaders can also fall into habits and patterns that drift over time. Everything over time tends to drift by nature. A small practice, carried out consistently over five years, can negatively impact leadership effectiveness. School leaders who always have to have the last word in a conversation, for example, can be overall very good at their jobs and, through this practice, hinder their school's culture. Being aware of these small habits is also important for established and effective school leaders.

Identifying Small Habits is intended to help all leaders identify a few habits in their own practice, reflect upon their patterns, and strategize around improvement. Leaders can read from cover to cover or pick and choose—and come back to—chapters that spark additional reflection. All leaders likely practice, to some degree, at least one of the thirty-eight small habits surfaced in this book. By identifying these habits and working towards improvement, leaders can bolster their own effectiveness while also providing their school and organization with the best versions of themselves.

Introduction

Jared is an elementary school principal entering his sixth year leading Emerson Elementary. Prior to his hire as building principal, Jared had worked in a neighboring district as a special education teacher and assistant principal. Overall, this is Jared's eighth year in school administration across multiple buildings and districts.

Needless to say, Jared is an experienced school leader. He learned from his early mistakes and has built solid relationships in his tenure. Student outcomes have trended in the right direction and staff tend to stay in the school despite opportunities to transfer to other schools or districts.

Over time, however, Jared has developed small habits that detract from his overall effectiveness. These habits, furthermore, are extensions of Jared's overall positive traits as a leader. For example, Jared is a highly organized building leader. He develops master schedules and staffing schedules well in advance and asks for input on their implementation. Sometimes, however, he finishes a schedule on a Friday evening and emails it to staff asking for feedback. Although he realizes that staff are spending time with their families after another long week, he wants to get it "out there" to demonstrate to staff his commitment to their input.

Despite these good intentions - and as an extension of Jared's commitment - the last thing his staff wants on a Friday evening is an email from their boss. Even though he is not expecting anyone to answer over the weekend, the email could have been drafted, saved, and sent at 8:00am on Monday morning when staff are arriving at work. This would have avoided staff having to consider their boss's email over their weekend. Although this is seemingly small, it does intrude on his staff's personal lives. Over time, if practiced consistently, this small communication habit may lead to some staff tuning out these emails.

Similarly, Melody is a highly-skilled district curriculum leader who has shepherded her district through multiple state-level changes. In her region, she is one of the longest-tenured curriculum leaders and a "go-to" for other districts when it comes to analyzing and implementing these changes. Few school leaders possess the skill set and expertise that Melody does on these issues.

In recent years, Melody's district has hired several new building principals who look to her for advice on these topics. While many administrators are at the front-end of their careers, Melody has only two years until retirement. Furthermore, the state has just introduced new standards in ELA and Math. This combination of new building administrators, Melody's career arc, and new state standards have merged in real-time.

While Melody would usually develop a multiyear implementation plan with broad staff input and feedback, these circumstances have led to Melody having a lack of patience with outcomes. Her usual implementation plans for a three-to-five year phase-in have been truncated into a much smaller time frame. This lack of patience with outcomes, although not interpreted by Melody as such, has caused her colleagues to push back against her current plan.

In both of these above examples, the school leader in question is experienced and successful. Both Jaren and Melody are respected leaders in their fields and have contributed to their district and region's knowledge-base. Both, however, are exhibiting small habits that detract from their effectiveness. In Jared's case, his urgency with planning and soliciting feedback is unnecessarily intruding into his staff's work-life balance. For Melody, her urgency over implementing new standards - in the face of her own career arc - is rushing an important standards change implementation in ELA and Math. In both cases, the individual school leader may not perceive how their actions are impacting others. Additionally, in both cases, remedying the situation does not entail dramatic changes on the leader's behalf.

Identifying Small Habits

This book is designed for leaders like Jared and Melody. Both are experienced, successful, and respected, yet developed small habits that they may not perceive as detracting from their effectiveness. The habits identified in both cases are also seemingly small; in and of themselves, they are not catastrophic. Yet, if practiced over time, they become leadership patterns that can have negative consequences.

Each chapter in this book identifies one of these small habits. Over the next thirty-eight chapters, habits are identified that often simmer below the surface for too long. Engaging in subtle favoritism over time, for example, can lead to cynicism and morale loss among a building. A leader may not even realize that they are engaging in subtle favoritism by discussing the football game with the same colleague each Monday morning. Other staff, however, may perceive such favoritism and begin to make connections that do not exist.

Engaging in subtle favoritism is one such example. Others include small habits around communication, self-care, professional relationships, and other topics. Each small habit may be difficult to perceive and as a one-off event, not problematic on the surface. When these one-offs develop into small habits, however, leaders need to intervene and make course corrections before they drift too far off course.

Even good leaders develop bad habits over time and even successful leaders have blind spots. While my first book, *Crisis Management: Effective Leadership to Avoid Early Burnout* was designed primarily for aspiring and early career leaders, this book seeks a wider audience. The aspiring leader, early career leader, and the veteran leader will all benefit from reflecting upon these small habits and their own leadership practices.

Each chapter identifies and unpacks one such small habit. The habit is surfaced and examples provided to bring it to life. Then, different strategies are presented to course-correct on this habit. Each chapter is short in nature and easily digestible. This book can be read cover-to-cover or picked through chapter by chapter in any order desired. It is also designed to be read once all the way through with leaders identifying habits that speak to them and returning to those chapters as needed.

Central to this book's premise is that despite even good leaders having bad habits, these habits can be surfaced and improved upon before they become too dramatic. The first step is identifying these practices in our own leadership. After that, leaders can get an outside perspective on how their habits are impacting their effectiveness and put improvements in place. The key is to surface and identify such habits as soon as possible before the seemingly small crack in one's leadership widens into larger chasms.

Continuous Improvement as a Leader

When I mentor aspiring and early career leaders, continuous improvement is a central message. Going from teacher to assistant principal, for example, requires developing additional skills. Then, being promoted from assistant principal to principal requires another leap in one's ability to lead. Each step up the ladder requires a larger array of skills. Leaders who lean on their previous experience to get them through larger challenges are mistaken. Success as a teacher does not guarantee success as an assistant principal. Success as an assistant principal does not guarantee success as a principal. And so on.

The important question to ask is "how can I get better?" Moving into a new position or a new district requires growth above and beyond what was needed for the prior step. Just because someone was a successful principal in one district does not mean that person will be successful in another district. Even hall of fame sports coaches have gotten fired from jobs. Leadership success is often contextual and requires even successful leaders to get outside of themselves and seek continuous improvement.

The next thirty-eight chapters should hit different leaders differently as they read on. Each individual habit may not apply to each individual reader. Over the course of all thirty-eight chapters, however, it is anticipated that leaders will see some of their practices reflected, both positively and negatively. Then, with that reflection, leaders can take the next steps towards becoming even better versions of their leadership selves.

Chapter 1

Being Inconsistent

When the principal sneezes, the entire building catches a cold. A leader's emotions, actions, what they do, and what they do not do, impact entire buildings and organizations in ways large and small. When staff have a clear picture of a leader's consistent, every day actions and values, strong cultures begin to grow.

Being in a leadership position is like constantly being on stage. Every word, every action, every emotion is on display. For many leaders, it takes time to be comfortable in this role. For some who were classroom teachers, they may have operated in relative isolation for many years. Closing the classroom door and teaching "my students" is far different from leading a group of professionals where most decisions have public implications.

Leading groups of people requires elevating above normal human reactions to events. Bringing home issues into work, allowing negative people to impact emotions, and other dynamics that cause people to run hot and cold cannot be allowed to hinder one's leadership. Getting better as a leader involves recognizing this fact and improving upon one's own ability to self-regulate in the face of adversity.

Even effective leaders may demonstrate inconsistency in small, yet subtle ways. Examples of these seemingly small, yet powerful ways include:

- A building principal who preaches personal connection, yet walks up and down the halls constantly answering emails on their phone.
- Leaders who rightfully address employee tardiness to work but often show up for their own meetings five to ten minutes late.
- Leaders who admonish students (and perhaps custodial staff) for not maintaining cleanliness while walking by trash in the hallways (and not picking it up).

In a leader's busy world, all three scenarios are understandable on the surface. Yet each slightly, over time, reinforces an inconsistent leadership pattern and can hinder morale. In fact, leaders who demonstrate these types of inconsistent behaviors may be very good administrators. They may be outstanding with students and stakeholders, highly organized, and empower staff to achieve terrific results. And still, they may be exhibiting inconsistent behaviors without fully realizing what is happening.

As a first step, leaders should reflect upon their leadership patterns. Patterns are different from intermittent events. Staff and stakeholders understand when leaders' lives are disrupted due to their own or a family member's illness. Every leader will have at least one meeting here and there where they are running late or will have moments when they are walking through the halls and the phone blows up. When these events become patterns, however, is when inconsistency can impact leadership effectiveness.

Being aware of subtle inconsistency is the first step. Then, there are specific strategies that leaders can employ to break down these barriers. First and foremost, leaders should be cognizant of how they are spending their time. Being late to meetings, showing up late for observations and leaving early, and similar events communicate that leaders are not on top of their own time management. All principals and other building and district leaders have more work to do than time in the day. However, prioritizing each day's work and structuring items in specific ways can be helpful.

For example, keeping Monday morning meeting-free may be a helpful strategy. Usually, Monday mornings and Friday afternoons tend to be busier than other points in the week. Being available to greet staff, wish students a good weekend, be at bus arrival and dismissal, and other events is important. Blocking off those strategic times—and perhaps others during the week such as student lunch and recess, when possible—can help leaders stay on top of their time.

Additionally, leaders should be aware of their own mental and emotional health. Being consistent and steady requires significant emotional energy. Maintaining emotions in the face of challenging people and dynamics is hard. Being able to get out of the public domain and recharge batteries is important. Then, coming back to that arena may meet with more success.

Asking others for feedback is also useful. While this approach may depend on a leader's trust with staff, gaining feedback from others helps leaders get out of their own heads and see issues from another's perspective. Often, leaders will need to ask more than once for staff and stakeholders to realize they are sincere. Being consistent in asking for feedback, moreover, helps leaders maintain congruence with what they're asking their teachers to do with students.

Finally, leaders should focus on making small progress each day rather than feel compelled to solve every problem at once. In baseball parlance, leaders should be singles hitters rather than home run hitters. While home runs are nice, they are often singular events. Making small progress each day—moving things along—is what contributes to success over time. Much of leadership success revolves around how leaders handle the seemingly small, mundane problems that creep up daily.

Being consistent in the small daily items leads to long-term success. For example, if leaders are consistently modeling picking garbage off the hallway floor, their message about maintaining cleanliness carries more meaning. Doing that consistently, over time, sends a strong message about what the leader values and makes it more likely that others will follow that example.

Too often, leaders focus on hitting the immediate home runs and neglect the small daily items that lead to long-term success. Planning a highly successful parent night, yet failing to show up to meetings on time, sends an incongruent message. Being consistent in the small daily practices over time is what truly moves the needle.

To reflect upon daily practices, leaders should ask themselves about areas in which they may say one thing, but sometimes practice something differently. Even if seemingly small, these daily practices, if incongruent with values, can erode leadership effectiveness over time.

Chapter 2

Relying Too Much on Email

They usually keep coming in bunches. Walk away from your desk and come back in ten minutes, and they seem to regenerate like a starfish's limbs—answer ten, and it seems like dozens more hit your inbox within a short time span. Email is a necessary component for all leaders and eats up large chunks of any leader's time on any given day. Relying too much on email to communicate, however, can have negative long-term effects for a leader's ability to build, sustain, and generate trust among constituents. It is also a bad habit that can be easy to fall into, and equally difficult to break.

The data around email practices among professionals is staggering. According to the Harvard Business Review (Plummer, 2019), professionals spend an average of 28% of their work day reading and answering emails. Encompassing 2.6 hours per day, that does not include time spent before work, in the evenings, and on weekends checking email either on a computer or a mobile device. Email on our smartphones only makes it easier to easily exceed that 2.6 hour mark on any given day.

Moreover, the study cites data that suggests that leaders receive over 120 new emails per day. And that was in 2019. Today, that number is likely higher. However, nearly two-thirds of those emails in the study were deemed "unimportant" and did not solicit a response. In addition, nearly 15% of those emails were either digital newsletters or marketing emails. It is no wonder that email is often cited as one of the top time-wasters for leaders when discussing time-management strategies.

While managing email as a time-management strategy is the subject for another chapter, it is easy to see how leaders can fall into bad habits around relying too much on email to communicate. Email is so voluminous and overwhelming that "getting emails out of the inbox" can help provide a sense of accomplishment. When leaders rely on email too much to communicate, however, it can hinder their ability to build trusting relationships.

Email is an ineffective communication tool for several kinds of interactions. First, email is one-dimensional and only conveys words on a screen.

5

It cannot convey tone, body language, or other empathic nuances that can be communicated over the phone or through face-to-face interactions. While more efficient, email tends to also beget more emails. Whereas a personal conversation can solve several issues in a short period of time, hashing out those types of concerns over email often leads to a back-and-forth that only clogs up inboxes.

Moreover, relying too much on email for communication—especially topics that require a personal conversation—often leads to the "tag-in effect." This happens when someone suddenly forwards an email to a third-party or CC's someone for whom the original email was not intended. When an email is sent, the sender immediately loses control of their message. After hitting send, control rests with the recipient, not the sender. The recipient can forward, CC, or even blind CC anyone at that point.

This can have negative long-term consequences. Often, we write emails for the original recipient, not for anyone else. Since email is one-dimensional and only conveys the written word, messages can easily become misinterpreted by the recipient and any third-party that is suddenly "tagged-in." This leads to several bad practices that can have negative consequences for trust-building relationships:

- Emails being forwarded to an unwanted third-party.
- Reply emails containing a CC recipient who was not on the original email, and for whom the original email was not intended.
- Individuals being blind CC'd without the original sender being aware.
- A third-party being CC'ed or blind CC'ed after several back and forths in the email thread.

None of the above practices build trust. In fact, being suddenly CC'd on an email chain and having to attempt to read through pages of past emails is frustrating, especially for those who supervise other leaders. Instead of communicating over email, the topic most likely warrants a phone call or a face-to-face conversation to tease out context, tone, and history.

Usually, thinking through a message's appropriateness for email is a good first step for leaders to consider. Email is an efficient communication tool for messages that fit a one-way communication need. Items such as reminders, notifications, and directives are often appropriate for email. Student concerns, parent communication, staff issues, and other topics laden with emotional and multiple interpretations are better-suited for more personalized communication. Misunderstandings that can result from one-dimensional emails can often be avoided through phone calls, video calls, or face-to-face conversations.

Leaders should evaluate their email habits to determine if they are relying on email too much to communicate. Are sent emails returned with unwanted third-parties "tagged-in?" Do leaders find that emails on the same topic are pinging back and forth with dozens of replies in a thread? If that's the case, then the topic warrants a phone call or a face-to-face interaction, not another email.

While it can feel good to clear an inbox and reply to everything that was received, leaders should take a step back and evaluate whether a reply is appropriate. Any topic that is subject to misinterpretation through one-dimensional communication should be a phone call or a meeting. Leaders will find that they can build trusting relationships through being consistent with these communication decisions rather than simply firing off another email that may or may not resolve the situation.

On any given day, relying too much on email is not detrimental to a leader's practice. Over time, however, this fault line can widen into a significant crack and lead to unwanted challenges. Relying too much on email to communicate often leads to leaders spending too much time in their office addressing emails; the more you send, the more you receive. Moreover, by spending too much time in the office, leaders fail to spend enough time having face-to-face interactions with their constituents. Relying too much on email leads to relying too little on other communication strategies that are much more effective at building trust.

What are your email practices? How many emails do you typically receive and send within any given day? Being more intentional about email practices can both save time in the long-run and build more trusting relationships.

Chapter 3

Talking about How Busy You Are

Entering into a career in school leadership will entail several trade-offs. Most importantly, it means that a school leader is responsible for larger swaths of the organization than they were in their prior role. This is not to say that teaching, or other pathways to school leadership, are not busy roles. The difference, however, is that the leader is responsible for managing other people and their outcomes, whereas an individual teacher can focus on their own students. Students, by and large, are much easier to work with than adults.

Therefore, an essential trade-off when going into leadership is that many more adults bring their wants, needs, and agendas to the table than in previous, student-focused roles. Furthermore, at the end of the day, the leader is responsible for managing those adults. This entails far more mental and physical time than many roles that lead to school leadership.

Understanding the essential trade-off that takes place can help mitigate another bad leadership habit: talking about how busy you are. Undoubtedly, you are busy as a school leader, but continually talking about it often rubs people the wrong way. In choosing the leadership position, salary, and responsibility, you are also choosing to be busier than you were in your previous role. Constantly talking about being busy is a bad leadership habit.

COMPLAINING ABOUT BEING BUSY

Talking about being busy can take two forms: complaining and humble bragging. Complaining is a very negative look for school leaders. There is a difference between complaining and venting to a trusted colleague. The latter is understandable and often productive; we all need to get things off our chest every once in a while. The former, however, comes off to staff as a sign of ineffective leadership.

School leadership entails being available and accessible to staff. This can be challenging considering how many people and issues can appear at once.

The school leader, however, would do well not to let their stress and anxiety around being busy translate into continual complaining. Staff often view a complaining leader as ineffective—"if they cannot handle lunch and recess, how are they going to handle bigger issues?" often gets asked. Rather than complain about being busy, school leaders should consider finding a trusting colleague who can help them manage those emotions when they appear.

BEING BUSY: "HUMBLE BRAGGING"

The other form that talking about being busy takes is humble bragging. Often, leaders view their talk about being busy as a status symbol. Research has demonstrated that bragging about being busy—the "humble brag"—detracts from leadership effectiveness and perception.[1] When leaders humble brag to make a positive impression on others, the strategy often backfires because it is overtly insincere. As modesty is a highly-valued leadership quality, bragging about being busy often detracts from perceived effectiveness by staff and stakeholders.

Humble bragging can take many forms, both large and small. On a large-scale, it can manifest itself when leaders openly talk to their staff about how busy they are in a way that reinforces their own importance. This can take place when leaders talk openly with staff about how busy they are intentionally to let employees know how much they have on their plates. While their plates are undoubtedly full, so are those for staff. Teachers, Aides, Monitors, Clerical, Custodial, and other employees are usually also incredibly busy and make far less money at the same time. While the leader's work may be more complex at times, it does not mean that others are less busy.

Humble bragging usually takes place on a small scale, however, and can manifest itself in ways in which the leader may be unaware. For example, when leaders continuously state to employees about how busy they are, what they are really saying is "how important" they believe they are. All employees are busy—follow a school lunch monitor around for their shift and it will be readily apparent how hectic that role is. While a school leader's job may be more complex than others, it should not be used as a measuring stick for other's busyness.

There are other small ways, as well, that school leaders may inadvertently communicate their busyness in a way that detract from their effectiveness:

- Having a consistent closed door for significant portions of the school day. While a closed door is necessary at times for confidential conversations, phone calls, or the necessary moments to get a little space, being inaccessible to staff sends the wrong message. Part of being the leader is being accessible to help people with their concerns.

- Discussing an area of professional growth in a manner that conveys false humility. For example, if a deadline is missed, a leader may blame "being so busy" or "focusing on the students in the building" rather than admitting a mistake was made. It is far better to own a mistake and apologize than to convey a sense of false humility about an area of professional growth.

In little ways, leaders may talk about how busy they are with their colleagues, staff, and supervisors in a manner that detracts from their actual or perceived effectiveness. It is better to realize that everyone is busy—monitors, teachers, bus drivers, clerical staff, cafeteria staff, aides, superintendents—than to single oneself out as being so busy that certain tasks cannot be completed.

Another unspoken facet about leadership and either complaining about being busy or engaging in humblebragging has to do with a pragmatic aspect of school leadership. Usually, the school leader is the highest paid employee in a building. While a 40-year veteran teacher may out-earn a building principal, it is uncommon for the building principal not to be the highest paid employee among immediate staff. As a practical matter, highly paid leaders should not complain about being busy. It is part of the trade-off when the job is accepted. In particular, staff earning minimum wage while performing labor-intensive tasks—1:1 Special Education Aides, main office support staff, cafeteria employees—do not want to hear about how the highly-paid leader is stressed or busy. While they may empathize with a momentary comment, leaders who consistently point out their hectic pace risk alienating their rank and file employees.

Leaders should differentiate between occasional venting to a trusted colleague and consistently talking about being busy to staff and supervisors. All leaders need trusted colleagues and mentors to seek advice from; it is a difficult profession. Consistently talking about being busy to staff and supervisors—whether complaining or promoting a false sense of humility—may detract from a leader's effectiveness.

All leaders should ask themselves, "when stressed or momentarily overwhelmed, do I project those emotions onto others, even implicitly?" Talking about how busy you are is a small leadership habit that leaders would be smart to correct as soon as possible.

Chapter 3

NOTE

1. Sezer, O., Gino, F., & Norton, M. I. (2018). Humblebragging: A distinct—and ineffective—self-presentation strategy. *Journal of Personality and Social Psychology, 114*(1), 52–74. https://doi.org/10.1037/pspi0000108.

Chapter 4

Failing to Give Gratitude

School systems are complex organizations and no one person leads an initiative, supports a program, or moves a data point by themselves. Leaders make a critical mistake if they fail to realize that everyone within the system plays a role in student success. This goes beyond the occasional "thank you" or end of year speech. Employees will notice if a leader falls into bad habits around failing to give gratitude.

Gratitude in organizations has been a highly-researched and complex topic. Research has indicated that gratitude occurs at several levels. At an organizational level, formal appreciation programs may be aligned to human resource initiatives. Moreover, at an individual level, leaders live "in the moment" with their staff and their attentiveness to needs, benevolence, and humility play a role in how gratitude is conveyed—or not. At an event level, leaders may express gratitude when disruptive events happen and staff members contribute to solving problems.[1] It is important for leaders to recognize that each level holds importance. Individual leaders will have more influence at certain levels depending on their organizational role.

Most gratitude likely occurs at the event level; a disruptive incident happens on the playground, and several monitors contribute to the solution. Likely, the leader will verbally thank their staff in those moments. While such thanks is more than merited, leaders should also consider the days when those disruptive episodes do not occur. More likely than not, the everyday efforts by staff members contribute to days when disruptive incidents do not occur. It is in these situations where leaders should pay close attention to giving gratitude.

"Persistent gratitude" results when staff feel a stable tendency towards feeling grateful within a particular context, in this case, the school system.[2] Creating a gratitude habit within a building or organization reinforces these emotions over time. Then, when events occur, staff have built an emotional schema within which to interpret events. All staff respond to their environment in myriad ways. When staff work in an environment where they feel valued, trusted, and thanked, they are more likely to want to give 100% in the workplace everyday.

Conversely, leaders who feel that employees should not be thanked for "doing their jobs" run a grave risk. While it is true that monitors are paid for maintaining playground safety and the lack of disruptive incidents should be expected, the job's emotional toll requires continual positive reinforcement. Working in a school system is emotionally draining work. Maintaining a positive emotional state in such a workplace requires leadership that understands how gratitude can influence perceptions and interpretation.

Even effective leaders may possess a bad habit around failing to give enough gratitude. Expressing thanks in the workplace may not come naturally to many school leaders. Bosses can be pleasant work for and still have room to grow in this area. Creating systems of persistent gratitude, however, is one major way to take a building or organization to the next level. Building and maintaining high performance in high-stress environments such as school systems requires an intentional focus on building such a culture.

There are several ways that leaders can improve their gratitude habit. The first is to walk in their employee's shoes. While tracking data, building master schedules, and other examples of technical leadership work are important, investing time to understand employee's challenges is also crucial. There's a reason why "Undercover Boss" was a hit television show. Leaders often do not understand the day to day complexities and challenges that encompass other positions within the system. Being present on the playground, getting into classrooms, and riding buses are all ways that school leaders can better understand the challenges that accompany other positions that contribute to school success.

Additionally, many leaders feel that they need to have a big moment to express thanks. Actually, the opposite is true. Leaders should praise staff and give thanks at every opportunity, no matter how small it may seem. It is more important to express regular thanks for incremental progress than to wait for "big wins." This is especially true with behavioral change. If there are staff members whose performance needs to improve, praising the earliest recognized improvement is critical. Praise builds momentum and lets the staff member know they are on the right path.

Finally, it is important for leaders to understand that gratitude exists on macro and micro levels. Building-wide, event-level gratitude builds collective efficacy. Additionally, gratitude should also be tailored to individual needs. General praise such as "thanks for all of your hard work" misses the mark. Rather, focus on the specific actions and tasks that contributed to overall success. Each staff member plays a specific role in the organization's success. Noticing and praising individual efforts goes a long way towards building relationships.

There are other small, habit-building practices that leaders can employ daily thanks that are cost-effective, efficient, and impactful:

- Establish a habit of sending one thank you card per day. Lay it out on your desk before you leave for the day, and make it the first task completed each morning.
- Leave blank thank you cards in the school mail room and encourage staff to take them and write thank you cards for their colleagues.
- Create a roster of all staff in your building and set a goal to talk to a specific number each week on a rotating basis. Thank them during that conversation. This will ensure that face-to-face thanks are being expressed to all staff as the year progresses.
- Find opportunities for staff to collectively support local causes. For example, organizing coat drives during winter months helps build a sense of collective gratitude among staff and helps the community.

Leaders who fail to give consistent gratitude miss out on critical opportunities to build a positive culture. In any organization, what gets noticed is what gets done. When leaders are intentional about noticing staff contributions and consistently giving thanks, they reinforce those behaviors and increase the likelihood that they will continue. And, on a more basic level, it is also the right way to lead. Part of leadership's challenge is to rise above the everyday angst and bring out the best in staff. Establishing a consistent gratitude habit is one major way to accomplish that goal.

When thinking about their habits around gratitude, leaders should ask themselves "am I building a culture of persistent gratitude with the structures that are currently in place?"

NOTES

1. Ryan Fehr, Ashley Fulmer, Eli Awtrey, & Jared Miller (2017). *The grateful workplace: a multilevel model of gratitude in organizations.* Academy of Management Review, Volume 42, No. 2, 361–381. https://doi.org/10.5.5465/arm.2014.0374.
2. Ibid.

Chapter 5

Inappropriate Social Media Use

Social media has opened multiple new avenues for school leaders to promote their school's identity, best practices, and celebrations. Particularly for communicating with stakeholders, it can be a powerful tool. Superintendents can communicate weather delays, principals can easily highlight student celebrations, and teachers can share best practices more readily than ever before. A quick scroll for educational leaders on Twitter will yield several examples of how savvy administrators have leveraged social media to develop positive narratives about their schools.

School leaders also possess more power than ever to promote their own personal and professional brands on social media. Endeavors such as professional development, conference attendance, and best practice sharing can lead to thousands of followers. Savvy school leaders can quickly build a professional learning network to not only tap into for professional learning, but also to promote their own brand as a lifelong learner.

With that access, however, comes potential pitfalls. It is just as easy to share inappropriate social media messages as it is to share professional highlights. For this chapter's purposes, "inappropriate" does not mean wholesale, character-destroying social media posts. Rather, this chapter focuses on potential social media habits where leaders may overshare information that detracts from their effectiveness. To understand how this small habit can impact leadership, it is important to understand why social media is a medium where oversharing may be viewed negatively.

Leaders should realize that online environments differ from face-to-face interactions. Whereas leaders can cater to their audience in face-to-face interactions, online environments lack the verbal and non-verbal cues that would normally provide a person with a read on their audience's expression and dynamics.[1] Messages that may be successfully conveyed in a face-to-face interaction may not translate into an online environment in the same way. This difference and dynamic is important for school leaders to fully understand before they dive into the social media world.

17

An additional difference between face-to-face interactions and those in an online environment is the nature of the interactions. In a face-to-face exchange, both parties participate in a live, synchronous give and take. Furthermore, that give and take has a natural conclusion as the conversation ends. In an online environment, both dynamics differ. First, social media exchanges typically are asynchronous. When a school leader posts on Twitter, for example, the post goes out to the world and people can interact with that post on their own timetable. Moreover, social media posts never expire unless specifically deleted. An inappropriate social media post remains in the digital world for all time, unlike a face-to-face conversation that has a natural conclusion.

With those pieces in mind, it is important for school leaders to understand that social media can be an effective branding tool—for both schools and self—and also an ineffective way to convey other points. Social media platforms are excellent ways for school leaders to demonstrate different sides of their leadership; they may post pictures of school events, celebrations, highlights, and other examples that may not be conveyed as well in more formal communication such as memos. With that more-informal approach, however, comes the potential for more unprofessional messages and oversharing of some personal information.

School leaders should be mindful of the example they set at all times with their leadership. This extends to social media and is heightened in a world where many people spend more time on their smartphones than they do in face-to-face interactions. It is easy for leaders to enter into informal exchanges over social media that may detract from their leadership effectiveness. Some examples of these potential interactions include:

- Oversharing vacation pictures or other events. While highlighting dedication to family can be a positive branding tool, leaders should be cognizant that the lifestyle they convey is appropriate for a building principal who is responsible for other people's children, for example. Not every vacation experience has to be shared on Facebook or Twitter.
- Engaging in inappropriate comments on other's posts. A political conversation at the dinner table among family is different from a public, asynchronous post that will be seen by thousands of people. School leaders have to work with mostly everyone, regardless of political views. Keep the more-controversial topics confined to face-to-face conversations with those you trust, if compelled to air opinions.
- Tagging staff or coworkers without their permission. It is okay to attend a social event with staff (i.e., a retirement party) and perhaps even have one drink (although opinions on this point also vary). Sharing pictures

and tagging staff with drinks in their hand, however, should be avoided by school leaders.

- Venting or complaining about school conditions on social media. Facebook, Twitter, and other social media platforms are not the mediums for which to express frustrations. Rather, find a trusted colleague or mentor for such conversations.

To utilize social media appropriately, there are several steps school leaders can take. First, it is important to separate personal and professional sharing. Some crossover is natural. As aforementioned, highlighting family can build trust with a school community and make the leader more relatable to parents and staff. Some vacation photos may be texted to family members to share an experience rather than posted on social media for the entire world to view. School leaders should be intentional about "why" they are using social media platforms. If a leader is using Twitter to highlight their school's best practices and celebrations—for school branding, not personal branding—it is important to maintain that narrative and not intersperse personal experiences that may appear out of place.

Second, leaders should be familiar with social media privacy tools. There are ways to set up a Facebook profile, for example, that does not entail the entire world viewing posts. Moreover, Twitter accounts can be set to private so only connections can view tweets. This can be an important privacy tool if a Twitter account is utilized more for personal posts than it is for professional branding. Furthermore, leaders should be intentional about who they are allowing as a connection. Just because a leader has a Facebook profile or a Twitter account does not mean that they need to accept connection requests from staff and stakeholders. It is still possible to be connected in the real-world and not connected in the social media world.

Finally, if a school leader is utilizing social media for their own professional branding, they should be aware of how colleagues and supervisors may perceive their activity. Many school leaders extend their professional influence beyond their day-job; many write books, host podcasts, engage in speaking events, and other avenues. If this is the case, it is important to be intentional about when those posts happen and how they are conveyed. Such personal branding should not happen during work hours and it should be clear that in those capacities, a leader is representing themselves and not the district for which they work.

Oversharing personal information, complaining on social media, inappropriately tagging colleagues and staff, and failing to be intentional about social media purposes are all bad habits that leaders should avoid. To determine whether a leader has fallen into these habits, they should explore their relationship with social media platforms and analyze their recent posts from the perspective of their supervisor, staff members, and parent community. An important question to ask for school leaders is, "is my social media presence conveying the professional image that I want to convey as an effective leader?"

NOTE

1. Vincent Cho and Jo Beth Jimerson (2016). *Managing digital identity on twitter: the case of school administrators.* Educational Management, Administration, & Leadership, pp. 1–17, DOI: 10.1177/1741143216659295.

Chapter 6

Making Hiring Decisions Based on Implicit Bias

Hiring decisions are among the most important that any leader will make. A thorough process for hiring that includes reference checks of past supervisors, in-depth interviews, and other follow-ups is critical. The failure to invest the necessary time for hiring well will lead to employment problems down the road.

When combing through stacks of resumes and applications, it is only natural for leaders to be drawn to similarities to their own background. Similar schools, common personal and professional connections, and familiar experiences are among the dynamics that can jump off a page. In a stack of papers, these familiarities often lead to implicit judgments that influence the overall hiring process.

While commonalities can help build a bridge, overemphasizing these dynamics may also lead to poor hiring decisions. Implicit bias in hiring—often considered only in a negative scope when factoring out candidates—can also lead to poor decisions with those that end up getting the job. Thinking that "they went to the same school as I did so they must be a good candidate" often leads to poor hiring decisions.

Formed outside our conscious awareness, implicit bias is the result of a lifetime of associations and connections that form habitual thinking patterns within our mind. Whether they are based on race, gender, ethnicity, common experiences, or other factors, these associations can be both positive and negative and influence our behavior and decisions. Recognizing this bias in our hiring practices is the first step towards rooting out this bad leadership habit.

Leaders who think they do not possess implicit bias are fooling themselves and doing harm to their schools. Implicit bias exists in everyone, even when it does not immediately come to the fore. The following examples are indications of implicit bias in hiring practices:

21

- After reading a resume and ascertaining that a candidate attended the same teacher prep program as the principal and had the same program advisor, a school leader calls the program manager for a reference. After a positive phone call, the candidate is offered a teaching position in the school without any further reference checks.
- When a monitor opening arises in a school building, an existing staff member approaches their principal and recommends a friend from their neighborhood. Looking to hire the position as quickly as possible, the friend is offered the job without going through the regular interview process.
- A teacher's child is graduating from college and looking for a teaching position. They are granted an interview due to this connection. While they may not end up receiving the position, their interview slot could have gone to another candidate who possessed stronger credentials without having such connections.

In the above cases, some hiring decisions undoubtedly end up well. The teacher from the same prep program, for example, may end up being as strong as their advisor stated on the phone. By applying the above patterns to the hiring process, however, school leaders are perpetuating the same attitudes, approaches, and thought processes that already exist within the building or organization. In the long-run, lacking diversity in thinking and staffing harms school systems.

Often, the word "fit" is used to justify such hiring decisions. Seeking out candidates who "fit" the school's culture and profile inherently introduces implicit bias into the process. Determining "who fits" is often a function of group bias that may go unrecognized unless explicitly brought to the forefront. Because "fit" can be determined differently by everyone, introducing this ambiguous concept into the hiring process can allow for an individual's implicit bias to affect hiring decisions.

When this criteria surfaces in an interview process, leaders should probe below the surface to ascertain "why" committee members feel that certain candidates are a good "fit" while others are not. More likely than not, this determination will have something to do with criteria that have little in common with the job duties; rather, they will be influenced by common connections, background, or attitudes.

School leaders can take strides to root out implicit bias in hiring decisions in several ways. First, establishing a common training for all interview committees—regardless of position—is a first step. Conducting awareness training at the interview processes beginning will help committee members understand how their own implicit biases may be favoring some candidates over others. Over time, if this training is implemented district-wide, it will become part of the organization's culture.

Part of the training should be the commitment to hold everyone accountable. Establishing team norms is critical. One norm should be that when a committee member hears someone else's implicit bias come out, it should be called out in a professional and respectful manner. For example, if someone says "I like candidate A because they went to this school, and they will know a lot of the staff already," such a comment should be surfaced as possessing implicit bias. Candidate A may be the best candidate for other reasons, but their familiarity with the school should not be the main reason.

Finally, hiring decisions should be made as objectively as possible and involve as much evidence as possible. If a candidate fails to list a past supervisor on a reference sheet, they should be asked to provide one. Demonstration lessons may be an integral part of the process to extend teacher interviews beyond 45-minute interviews. If possible, administrative candidates should visit faculty meetings and present to the entire staff as a finalist step. It can be difficult during the hiring process to simulate the day-to-day work that exists within a school. Getting candidates as close to that work as possible for evidence is one way to move beyond implicit bias influencing hiring decisions.

Getting beyond implicit biases and making hiring decisions based on objective evidence and data is important. Surfacing implicit biases, calling them out in a respectful manner, and getting candidates as close to the work as possible during the process are all important steps. Leaders should be on the lookout for recurring staff concerns that seemingly always arise. If staff are consistently sending the same students to the office, having the same students sit out at recess, and engaging in less-than-productive conversations with the same families, there may be some level of implicit bias in the system.

When hiring, leaders should ask themselves "why do I feel this is the best candidate and am I making that determination based on objective evidence and feedback?" When leaders model this process over time, it is likely that such thinking patterns will become part of the organization's culture.

Chapter 7

Conflating Authority
with Influence

Earning "the title" or "the office" can be an exciting step on the leadership journey. Hard work and dedication are involved in earning that first leadership position or climbing the ladder into positions of greater responsibility. There are fundamental differences between teaching younger students and leading older adults. Understanding this dynamic rests on understanding the difference between authority and influence.

There are many structural pieces to teaching younger students that emphasizes authority over influence. It is not that great teachers rely on their authority; usually it is the opposite. Rather, elements in the system reinforce the teacher's authority, or the principal's authority, over the student. Dynamics such as test scores, marking period grades, scheduling forces, and others dictate that authority rests with the adults and not with students.

Leaders make a mistake when they bring this mindset into their leadership work with adults. The playing field is much more level. Especially in states with strong collective bargaining groups, school districts and unions are often legally required to negotiate in good faith on mandatory issues. Moreover, many veteran teachers will have had several principals and district-level leaders in their careers. Many teachers will last in their schools longer than their leaders. These two dynamics tend to level the playing field when it comes to authority's true worth in leadership roles.

Effective leaders recognize that authority is a valuable tool and exercise it judiciously when needed. There are times when authority must be used. Health and safety issues, and other situations where student success is at risk come to mind. This should be used sparingly, however. More often than not, a power play attempted over school staff leads to mistrust and poor working conditions.

It is possible to hold the title, sit in the office, have a fancy business card, and still not possess influence. Authority does work to compel compliance in many situations. Even unhappy staff often go along with a power-hungry leader because it is just easier than trying to fight back on every decision. There are a series of indicators that reflect whether leaders recognize the difference between authority and influence.

One important dynamic involves recognizing others. Leaders who build influence relentlessly praise others and recognize their staff's hard work. This is not a once-in-a-while occurrence. Every building has incredible staff who go above and beyond every day. Leaders who recognize this and praise not only the extraordinary work but the valiant, ordinary efforts build influence.

Influence is also built through empowering others. Trust and respect are earned when leaders recognize that they themselves do not hold all of the answers. If a school building is having issues on their playground, the school monitors would be an essential group to consult. When leaders try to impose ideas from above, cynicism reigns. When they ask for other's input and empower them to be part of the process, influence builds.

Finally, influence leaders always lead with their staff's health and wellness in mind. Rather than use their authority to coerce a teacher to take an extra duty or teach an extra class, they engage staff in conversations about what is and is not possible. Even the most above-and-beyond staff members have their limits. Influence leaders are mindful of burning out their employees and always think deeply about how the work is organized.

Relentlessly praising, empowering, and prioritizing health and wellness are three ways that leaders build influence. Those who are intentional about this process recognize that influence is necessary to move any school or district forward. Conversely, there are telltale signs of leaders who emphasize their authority or conflate the two.

Leaders who emphasize their personal authority are likely to take credit for successes that may not be their own doing. When test scores in a building rise, for example, leaders certainly had a role but classroom teachers were the ones directly performing the work. Additionally, these leaders likely overuse "I" as a pronoun when talking about their school, their community, and their successes. The reality is that no one person can do it alone. The room is always smarter than any one individual.

Similarly, leaders who emphasize their authority are focused solely on just getting the work done. The schedule needs to be made, and the principal likely has the authority to finish it. Therefore, teachers teach what they teach and that is that. Little consideration is given to how teachers or staff would feel about these assignments or if they are made with an eye towards putting staff in a position to be successful. The schedule is complete. While principals have the authority to complete tasks in this way, they break trust and fail to build influence when doing so.

The reality is that administrators who lead with influence are going to be busier and more sought-after than those who lead with authority. Students, staff, and stakeholders approach those whom they think can help them or just listen to their concerns. Self-serving leaders who emphasize their authority are likely not ones they seek out. While stressful at times, being someone staff turn to in order to help make the school and organization better is a tremendous compliment. It shows that students, staff, and stakeholders recognize the leader as one who empowers others and realizes they do not have all of the answers all of the time.

While often hidden below the surface, this difference between authority and influence can make or break leadership success. Over time, leaders who fail to build influence or conflate the two dynamics contribute to a learning environment trending towards less trust and collaboration. On the other hand, leaders who relentlessly praise, empower others, and demonstrate humility and vulnerability lay another brick towards a trustworthy school.

For those who have earned their first position or continue to move up the ladder, conflating authority with influence may appear through small habits such as overusing "I" when talking about school success. These habits may not be egregious to the point where the leader's job is in question. Rather, recognizing these dynamics and making small corrections can help leaders improve upon their own practice.

There may not be one overarching question that uncovers this often-hidden dynamic. Rather, close attention to the building's culture may be helpful. Those with influence are often those whom others seek out in times of need. Who are those staff members? And, more importantly, is the leader with the most formal authority one of them?

Chapter 8

Neglecting Mental and Physical Self-Care

The most important gift a leader can give to their school community is a physically and mentally healthy self. Too often, however, leaders try to take care of everyone but themselves and de-prioritize their own mental and physical health. On many levels, it is an understandable phenomenon. Most school leaders pursue administrative positions because they want to help people and help students succeed; their own mental and physical health often comes second to everyone else's.

This chapter's message is not to neglect leadership's higher calling. Accepting a leadership position requires trade-offs; one of those trade-offs is that the leader is required to care for their stakeholders. Principals, in particular, are thrust into the middle of their staff and student's lives. It is one of the position's true blessings, but also a challenge that should be managed properly in order that the leader does not burn out unnecessarily.

On top of those challenges, leadership is often a lonely endeavor. More often than not, peer groups do not carry over into transitions from staff positions to leadership positions. This can be especially true for leaders who are promoted from within an organization. Explicit and implicit boundaries may exist between staff and administration that leaders promoted from within an organization's staff ranks should consider. The key is to perceive one's role and power in a manner that promotes leadership resilience rather than damages physical and mental well-being.[1]

Taking care of one's physical and mental well-being is a task that can easily track off course. Small daily habits, if neglected, can compound over time into large-scale challenges in this area. Not getting enough sleep, failing to properly manage stress and anxiety, consistently eating unhealthy foods, and related topics may be manageable in small quantities, but over time can lead to major problems. All leaders have stressful stretches where physical and mental health and work-life balance are out of whack. There is a difference, however, between a short stretch of time and long gaps neglecting these areas.

Neglecting mental and physical health can occur in several areas. Below are just a handful of topics for which better habits can impact leadership effectiveness:

SLEEP HABITS

According to a 2018 Harvard Business Review article, the percentage of Americans getting no more than six hours of sleep per night rose from 22% in 1985 to 29% in 2012. Furthermore, an international study cited in 2017 reported that among leaders who reported their sleep patterns, 42% reported getting less than six hours of sleep per night.[2]

Poor sleep habits and their impact on physical and mental well-being for the leader themselves has been well-documented. Leaders, however, should also be aware that their poor sleep habits may also spill over onto their subordinates. Barnes also found that when leaders developed poor sleep habits, they were more likely to exhibit poor leadership qualities among their teams.[3] These qualities included expressing frustration more readily and abusive behaviors, which in turn led to lower motivation levels among subordinates.

Furthermore, when leaders sleep poorly and decide to work late into the night or send a few emails to get ideas off their minds, there is a spillover effect on staff. When teams wake up to find that their leader was emailing them at 3am, there may be an implicit message that subordinates feel their boss is expecting them to also work during those times. Not only does poor sleep habits harm the leader themselves, but it may also harm their team's overall effectiveness. There are small ways that leaders can prioritize their sleep habits, including:

- Develop a habit of putting the phone down after 9pm, unless an emergency arises.
- Be honest with yourself: there is not anything on TV after 9pm that is better than getting more sleep; if there is, invest in DVR.
- Prioritize getting fresh air, when possible, before bed and/or first thing in the morning.

FAILING TO MAINTAIN WORK-LIFE BALANCE

Many leaders fail to maintain work-life balance because they attempt to be all things to all people all of the time. In leadership positions, the work is never done: there is always one more email to send, one more phone call to make, and one more task to complete. A school leader could spend 24 hours per day at their job and, most likely, never feel like the work is "done." Therefore, it can be easy for leaders to slip into bad habits around failing to maintain work-life balance.

Most importantly, leaders should consider the "life" portion of the work-life balance equation. The work is always there, but the "life" will not be after a period of time. Children are young for a finite period of time while there will always be principal openings. Families only have a set number of vacations together over the year while Superintendent positions will continue to open over time. Taking a position of higher pay and authority that may gratify the professional ego should be weighed against the costs to those children and family opportunities. The career ladder will be there, but the family opportunities may not be.

School leaders should consider these concepts within both their current job and for potential career opportunities. It is far better to remain in a current position that supports work-life balance than jump to an opportunity that demands that "work" take undue precedence over "life." Having conversations with family, doing timely "self-audits" to ensure priorities are in place, and creating professional boundaries at work are all good steps leaders can take in this area. Other potential steps could be:

- Conduct a time audit for a week and analyze the results; what does your time look like in terms of work-life balance?
- Have honest conversations with family. There are points during the school year where work demands increase. Communicate these ahead of time with family and promise to pay it back twofold.
- Analyze career opportunities and de-prioritize how a career jump will gratify professional ego. Those opportunities will be there down the road if leaders continue to succeed in their current position.

OVERINDULGING IN ALCOHOL

With additional stress also brings additional need to practice self-care. Unfortunately, those stressors may also lead to unhealthy coping habits including an overindulgence in alcohol to unwind. Although it can begin in small ways, bad habits around alcohol consumption can easily form over time. A leader does not need to self-identify as an alcoholic or be seeking professional help to struggle with this topic.

What can begin with one or two drinks on a Friday evening can develop into habits that have long-reaching impacts. This focus is not upon alcoholism as a disease or even for those who need to seek some level of professional help. A few bad habits in this area, rather, can have negative impacts on leadership.

Leaders should engage in self-reflection around their relationship with stress relief and alcohol. Questions that leaders should ask themselves may include:

- How many nights a week is alcohol consumed?
- Is alcohol a "go-to" on a consistent basis to "wind down" at the end of a long workday?
- Does alcohol consumption the previous night ever lead to groggy work mornings?
- Has a family member ever observed that alcohol consumption is interfering with family life, such as being a good spouse and parent on weekends?

This section simply asks leaders to evaluate their relationship with alcohol and pay attention to its impact on their work and family life. Leadership is a stressful endeavor and it is important to be cognizant that bad habits around alcohol can impact effectiveness without becoming a full-blown professional crisis.

IF IT WOULD HELP, SEEK HELP

Even the world's best athletes have coaches. School leaders should be willing to seek someone to talk to, such as a leadership coach, if needed. Often, a leadership coach can help leaders develop positive habits. However, if challenges exist around lack of sleep, work-life balance, and alcohol consumption, more professional help should be sought. Most employee agreements have some level of Employee Assistance Program support and are confidential. Leaders should ask themselves, what areas around mental and physical self-care should I focus on to benefit my personal and professional life?

NOTES

1. Adam Waits, Eileen Choi, Joe Magee and Adam Galinsky. "Not so Lonely at the Top: The Relationship Between Power and Loneliness. *Organizational Behavior and Human Decision Process*, (2015), 130, 69–78.

2. Christopher Barnes, "Sleep Better, Lead Better," *Harvard Business Review*, September 2018, pp. 140–143, https://hbr.org/2018/09/sleep-well-lead-better.

3. Ibid.

Chapter 9

Avoiding Difficult Conversations

Among the most challenging dynamics when moving from teacher *within* the system to leader responsible *for* the system is having difficult conversations. A new principal, who served as a classroom teacher for 15 years, is not responsible for the system for the first time. Not that individual teachers are not responsible for the system's success, but they are not responsible for holding others accountable who are falling short.

Moreover, many leaders—especially at their career's beginnings—are people pleasers. They enter into leadership because they want to help people. Building positive relationships is part of that journey, and experience with difficult conversations may be an area lacking initially from a new leader's skill set. Instead of having the necessary conversation, behaviors continue to negatively impact the team's performance.

This does not mean that leaders should go around their building or organization and engage in difficult conversation after difficult conversation. As leaders build relationships in their buildings, they will begin to perceive where the leverage points exist. There are situations, however, that warrant a difficult conversation. These may include:

- Situations where one team member's lack of performance is impacting other's ability to their jobs. For example, if a lunch monitor is consistently late for their shift, the supervisory burden for more students is shifted onto the other monitors. This not only is not fair to them, but also compromises student safety,
- Instances where certain staff have consistently poorer outcomes than their peers. For example, if one reading teacher among a team of five interventionists consistently has fewer students gaining levels, a conversation into "why" may be warranted.
- Behavior that is so egregious that it has to be confronted. In these situations, employment norms or agreements have been violated to such an

extent—and perhaps publicly—that *not* addressing the situation would have a detrimental impact on the leader's effectiveness.

Recognizing the behavior or situation is the first step; actually addressing it can be more challenging. Research has demonstrated that when leaders anticipate or encounter disagreement, the conversations are likely to be stressful and ineffective.[1] Because of this, leaders are likely to put off such conversations or not fully address the situation. Often, leaders will raise the issue to the point of noticing with the employee, but fall short of actually holding the employee accountable. There are several reasons this may occur, which could include:

- Being uncomfortable with vulnerability. Many people are not comfortable with conflict and try to avoid it. This can be especially true for leaders who are people-pleasers and seek comfort and consensus at all costs.
- Lack of time. There is always too much to do, and putting off a difficult conversation that could take time is one way to rationalize delaying the discussion.
- Rationalizing the behavior away. Some employees are still effective at their jobs despite exhibiting these behaviors, although their behavior may erode team performance. Moreover, some employees are close to retirement or leaving the system anyway. They may "hang on" for another year or two while avoiding the need to have the difficult conversation.

While there are many reasons to avoid these conversations, doing so only allows the situation to grow. In some cases, the employee may perceive that their behavior will be tolerated and will continue. In other cases, employees may not realize that their performance or behavior is having a detrimental impact on the team. The lunch monitor may not realize, for example, that being late five minutes can have negative repercussions on colleagues and student safety.

Furthermore, many leaders avoid the difficult conversation because they do not possess the skill set to carry it out. There are strategies that leaders can employ to guide the conversation towards a "less difficult" place. While this may not avoid all discomfort that can occur, having a specific game plan for such conversations can be beneficial.

First, leaders should be cognizant that a trusting relationship always helps with challenging conversations. If employees know they are valued and supported, they are more likely to frame the leader's feedback in a helpful tone rather than an accusatory one. The difficult conversation should never be the first conversation that takes place. Walking alongside staff in their jobs and supporting their performance is a necessary first step towards earning that relational trust.

Moreover, addressing the behavior need not start with a difficult conversation. There will be situations so egregious that it may be unavoidable, but in many cases leaders can observe behavior and provide supportive coaching feedback at first. For example, in the case of the late lunch monitor, being in the cafeteria and seeing the employee consistently enter late can lead to an initial support encounter. Asking if the employee and their family are okay, if an earlier time shift would be beneficial, or other ways to provide support are good first steps. This also lets the employee know that the leader is aware they are late, but in a supportive context.

While providing support, collecting as much objective data as possible is important. Objective data describes the behavior in a way that attempts to remove emotion. For example, having day-by-day evidence of arrival times takes the monitor's lateness out of the emotional realm and frames it objectively. It becomes less about the person, and more about the behavior. Leaders should always support the person and help them maintain their dignity even when having to have difficult conversations about behavior and performance.

If those supportive conversations fail to help the employee improve, a more direct conversation may be warranted. This is the "difficult conversation" that leaders so often avoid. At this stage, however, the employee should not be surprised the issue is being raised. Armed with objective data and prior supportive conversations, the leader is well-positioned to make their case. The goal of these conversations is improvement; many employees will demonstrate that they "get it" and will attempt to change course. If this is an ongoing pattern, moreover, it may be beneficial to memorialize the conversation in a follow-up memo. Having written evidence for these conversations and their outcomes may be important if the behavior does not change.

Even with the best laid plans, of course, many conversations will turn negative. Many employees will continue to rationalize their behavior and appear to not understand why it is problematic. If the employee becomes accusatory during the conversation, it may be helpful to have an additional person in the room. Many employees may want to bring union representation, and this should be granted. If the leader has provided support and has objective data, having others in the room may be beneficial.

Finally, it may be necessary to sever ties with an employee if these behaviors continue, or become more problematic. While leaders may feel bad that it has gotten to this step, they should take solace with their process. Providing support and coaching feedback will resonate with most employees, but not all. It is not worth the detrimental impact to a building or organization to keep an employee who clearly does not want to address their behavior. It is better to sever the relationship and incur the employee's enmity rather than enable problematic behavior that brings down an entire group.

Avoiding difficult conversations is natural for leaders who seek to avoid conflict. Leaders should consider the price that is paid when bad behavior and poor performance is allowed to continue unabated. Leaders should ask themselves—why are difficult conversations stress-inducing and what steps can be put in place to guide them in a positive direction?

NOTE

1. Robinson, V. M. J., Sinnema, C. E., & Le Fevre, D. (2014). From persuasion to learning: An intervention to improve leaders' response to disagreement. Leadership and Policy in Schools, 13(3), 260–296. doi: 10.1080/15700763.2014.922997.

Chapter 10

Engaging in Subtle Favoritism

It is natural for anyone—leaders included—to like some people more than others. We share more common interests with some people than others. Moreover, there are some people that are just plain challenging to be around. This can include those who leaders supervise, and it is natural that leaders will like some of their employees more than others on a personal level.

This can become problematic, however, when leaders let on that they do like some staff more than others. This can be done in obvious and not-so-obvious ways. Leaders who dole out favors and choice assignments based on their personal preferences do their entire organization a disservice. In addition, those leaders will likely be so overt in their favoritism that calls to be reigned in will occur.

These are not the leaders for whom this chapter is written. If leaders are showing overt favoritism and communicating their personal likes and dislikes through job rewards, a whole different set of remedies apply through district action. Rather, this chapter is written for leaders who are cognizant that overt favoritism is wrong, yet play favorites in more subtle ways that may be difficult to identify at first glance.

These subtle, yet powerful, ways that even effective leaders may play favorites often deal with their time, attention, and camaraderie. When this occurs as a pattern over time, other staff may pick up on it and begin to make connections that do not exist that can harm building and organizational culture. Some examples of these under-the-radar ways leaders may show favoritism include:

- A male elementary school principal spends every Monday morning talking about the football game with the two other male employees in the building in the mail room.
- During staff lunch, the Assistant Principal often eats with the same two or three staff members whose children also play on the same youth sports team.

- A building principal with both veteran and new staff is observed investing more time in new staff—that they themselves hired—and avoids the classroom of those staff whom they inherited.

In the above examples, malicious intent is likely not at play. The principalship is a stressful job, and talking about the football game on Monday may be seen as a way to get into the work week in a positive tone. Similarly, administrators and staff whose children are going through similar experiences will naturally have several things in common to talk about. Finally, a building principal may see those as "their staff," since they personally hired them, and want to invest in them since they believe both will be there for a long time.

These types of patterns, however, carried out over time, may have a negative effect on school culture. Staff who are not involved in these conversations or not "in the know" may begin to feel devalued. Furthermore, when some work assignments or other choices have to be made, staff may read into them intentions that are not there. For example, if the new teachers are the ones getting the first crack at the latest technology, those veteran teachers who have been in the building a long time may feel like the principal is playing favorites.

In these subtle ways, even good leaders can demonstrate patterns that point to favoritism towards some over others. The leader's time, attention, and camaraderie are valuable commodities, and leaders should be cognizant of how they are utilizing those resources. If leaders are spending too much time with some staff, or perceived as being chummy with some staff over others, perceived favoritism by others will likely be a result.

In reality, some employees are more likely, more relatable, and will likely be with the organization longer than others. These favoritism patterns, however, have the potential to simmer below the surface and promote cynicism among staff. What's worse, they often lead to staff divisions among the so-called "have" and "have nots" when it comes to the leader's perceived feelings towards employees.

There are specific strategies leaders can employ to guard against subtle, yet detrimental, favoritism practices. First, being aware that everyone has tendencies to play favorites is important. Leaders should be reflective enough to step out of themselves and attempt to perceive how their time, attention, and camaraderie is distributed. Putting systems in place to visit every classroom each day, greet all staff members as they enter the building in the morning, and build relationships across employee groups is crucial.

Additionally, leaders should be cognizant of how assignments are distributed among staff. Just because some staff are better than others at handling challenging students, for example, should not determine who is assigned where. Similarly, avoiding early morning assignments because—like the leader—a staff member has younger children will be perceived as favoritism. Delineating duty assignments, contractual obligations, and the like on a fair and equal basis is important. At times, some staff will need different accommodations than others. If leaders have avoided subtle favoritism, their staff will likely recognize this as being accommodating rather than playing favorites.

Moreover, leaders should build personal and professional relationships with all team members, especially those whom they do not particularly like. Often, these disagreeable staff members have important insight into building and organizational practices. Valuing their input and liking them personally are two different things. One strategy leaders can employ in this area is to list all staff members in the building, and make a conscious effort to engage in conversation with five different staff members each day, on a rotating basis. In this way, leaders can ensure that they are engaging all staff in personal and professional conversation.

Finally, leaders should attempt to get an outside perspective on their practices. This can be useful for several reasons, not just to avoid subtle favoritism. Asking a trusted colleague, mentor, or coach to sit in on meetings and provide feedback on how the leader's time, attention, and camaraderie are distributed may be insightful. Moreover, a trusted staff member in the building could also provide valuable feedback on these practices.

While overt and unethical favoritism does happen, this chapter focused more on the subtle ways that playing favorites can be detrimental to a leader's effectiveness. Moreover, it can have a negative impact on building and organizational culture. Leaders should ask themselves "is my time, attention, and camaraderie distributed evenly throughout the building, and if not, what practices can be put in place to make it so?"

Chapter 11

Trying to Always Win an Argument

As leaders, our viewpoints, decisions, and opinions are going to be constantly challenged by those we respect and those we do not. Many times, people will want to engage in an argument for the simple fact that they want to try to get one up on the boss. Other times, a leader's decisions run headlong against deeply-held convictions by others. In all cases where an argument may ensure, leaders should pause and think about whether an argument is worth having, before even thinking about if it is worth winning.

Leaders who engage in arguments about various policies, procedures, and practices often waste their precious energy on issues that matter little in the grand scheme of things. Many leaders will have worked for or with other leaders, staff, or stakeholders who seemingly have to get the last word or the upper hand in all discussions. Reflecting upon these experiences, most leaders will come to the conclusion that interacting with such people is exhausting and energy-sapping.

Leaders who engage in incessant arguing or having to have the last word in all conversations will quickly wear out their welcome. Even when staff and stakeholders have good ideas that could advance the organization, they will realize that bringing this idea to their supervisor will likely result in a one-sided conversation. Rather than being heard, the person will likely walk away having been told why their idea is not as good as the supervisor's idea.

When this pattern persists over time, staff and stakeholders stop contributing ideas. It is easy for staff and stakeholders to smile politely and feign consent rather than engage in healthy dialogue with such leaders. The worst thing a leader can do is shut down feedback loops that can lead to continuous improvement. Having to win every argument and always have the last word is a surefire route to this destination.

This is often a difficult habit to perceive in oneself. Asking for feedback from a trusted mentor or engaging in leadership coaching is one way to tease this out. Because the results of this habit—people *not* coming forward with thoughts and ideas—is passive, it can go undetected. A principal who lays out a ten-point plan to raise test scores at a faculty meeting and receives little to no feedback may believe their ideas were met with universal acclaim. Hidden within that silence, however, may be a staff that is worn out by the principal's consistent need to win every argument and have the last word.

Silence does not imply agreement and consent does not mean consensus. In the situation outlined above, it is just as likely that staff will smile and nod, and then return to their classrooms and continue down the same path. The missed opportunity here is for a consensus-building experience where the entire staff provides input and feedback. To do so, however, trust must exist where staff and the leader realize that their own ideas will be challenged by others.

Often, leaders engage in this bad habit because they believe their ideas are the right ones. They want to "do what's best for kids" and paint staff resistance not as an opportunity to build consensus but as pushback. After all, the administrator has additional advanced degrees and is certified to be a building principal, a director, or hold such a leadership position. Leaders who conflate their positional power with influence, however, do themselves little favors.

Rather, leadership's unique opportunity rests in being positioned to solicit feedback and craft ideas among broad stakeholder groups. A Superintendent, for example, sits as the organization's apex and can reach across to community leaders, building-leaders, staff, parents, and regional groups to test out an idea. The power does not rest in *having* the positional power; rather, the power lies in having access to broad groups to craft consensus around vision, mission, and goals. Leadership's true gift is being able to reach more people, not being able to make more unilateral decisions.

Leaders who recognize this likely feel they do not need to win every argument or have the last word. They recognize that their own ideas are a work in progress. They are not fully formed and only become better with input from others. Leadership is not about "arrival," it is about "destination." Getting to the destination is always a more rewarding journey when leaders realize that they need other's ideas and opinions much more than they need to protect their own.

The best way to win an argument, therefore, is to avoid one altogether. When someone challenges an idea, rather than see it as an invitation to engage in argument, it should be viewed as an opportunity to solicit feedback. Vision, mission, and goals should be developed collaboratively with stakeholder ownership rather than handed down from above by a leader with positional power. When viewed through this lens, it is likely that leaders will recognize that most arguments that can take place need not occur at all.

There are some areas, however, where a leader can and should engage in some argument. Not all ideas are created equal. Unfortunately, we still live in a society where some people want to erect barriers for student success. When these issues arise and directly conflict with mission, vision, and goals, leaders should take a firm position. They should not feel that they need to *win* an argument because, likely, people who hold such views cannot be convinced otherwise. Rather, standing up for students and their opportunities are victories in and of themselves.

Ultimately, leaders should also consider their interaction's purpose. There is no such thing as a neutral interaction—each interaction either leaves the other person a little better or a little worse off. Having to win every argument and always have the last word will inevitably leave people a little worse off consistently over time. There is a difference between simply stating one's viewpoint and then having to try to convince the other person of that viewpoint. The former is admirable, the latter usually a waste of time and energy.

If leaders are not receiving open feedback from staff and stakeholders, they should ask themselves "am I trying to always win an argument and have the last word?" Flipping this habit on its head and welcoming opportunities for input can be one step towards building a better organizational culture.

Chapter 12

Devaluing Support Staff and Their Impact

Often, within a school building, only a small handful of administrators are present. Many times, there may be only one—the building principal. While there are dozens of teachers, support staff also comprise a large percentage of adults within a building. These key contributors—clerical, maintenance, aides, monitors, cafeteria staff, bus drivers, among others—play a critical role for both the building's success and that of the building leader. Leaders who fail to properly value their support staff and their impact do so at their own peril.

Support staff impact student success in several ways. Often, they are the "eyes and ears" of a school as the staff who the community interfaces with the most. For example, bus drivers are often the first school employee to see students in the morning and the last to see them when the day is complete. When parents and guardians call the school or come to the school, they are greeted by clerical staff in the main office. When the building hosts after-school activities and community events, the maintenance staff has a large hand in setting up rooms and working with parents and guardians.

When students are fed on time, the building and its grounds are clean, and recess proceeds in an orderly manner, support staff are likely to thank. While the principal is leading data huddles or conducting observations, others are playing key roles. A principal can lead those sessions uninterrupted only when the other key players in the building are doing their jobs. An effective clerical staff, for example, can interface positively in the main office with families and does not need the principal's intervention as often.

These impacts may not be visible to leaders who are laser-focused on teaching and learning. That focus is well-placed, but leaders would do well to take a step back and think through their support staff's impact on the greater school community. In many cases, support staff live within the school district at greater rates than teachers or administrators. Their opinion of the school, of the leadership, and of the culture resonates throughout the entire community. Their opinion on the school budget, for example, holds considerable weight within the district. And often, their impact is not easily visible when all is going well.

There are several ways that staff can demonstrate their support staff's value beyond the occasional thank you or other gesture. Walking in the support staff's shoes is one pathway. Leaders should ride school buses, be present at lunch and recess, participate in feeding students, and help tear down school events with their maintenance staff. While leaders are busy and may not be able to do this every day, walking in their shoes will go a long way towards building trusting relationships with support staff. It demonstrates that these jobs have value, and that the leader recognizes the important role they play.

In addition, listening to support staff and their ideas for school improvement is important. For example, if a school is struggling with student management during recess, the employees with the best perspective are probably the ones who are closest to the issues. School monitors who are with students every day on the playground will have ideas on how to improve these processes. Holding regular meetings with support staff to demonstrate their value and listen to their ideas is critical. Leaders should develop a schedule for these meetings and communicate it early in the year. Often, it may entail some overtime for hourly employees, but this is a worthwhile investment. To build trust, gain perspective, and garner ideas is easily worth an hour of overtime for support staff.

Finally, leaders should publicly communicate their support staff's value at every opportunity. When introducing the band before a school concert, leaders can also thank their maintenance staff for setting up the stage. If parents and guardians are allowed to eat lunch with students, the leader can thank aides and monitors in the moment for their work. With digital and print media, leaders can communicate thanks and value through newsletters, weekly messages, and other avenues. It has never been easier to demonstrate support staff's value through these messages.

Walking in their shoes, listening to their input, and communicating their value are three ways that leaders can value their support staff and honor their impact. There are other, smaller ways that leaders should invest in, as well, including:

- Researching your association's School-Related Professionals Day (as it is called in New York State). Formally and publicly celebrating support staff and their impact on this day demonstrates that a leader is in tune with their needs.
- Include support staff on building-wide and district-wide committees such as the safety team, building planning team, and other shared

decision making platforms. Likely, support staff will bring a valuable perspective to solutions that other staff members may not have. A school safety team, for example, is likely not complete with a playground monitor or main office staff member.

- Find opportunities for teachers and support staff to get to know one another and build relationships. These events can be more-formal such as an end-of-year luncheon or informal. The more different staffing groups get to know each other and build trusting relationships, the less likely the leader will have to navigate interpersonal conflict among employees.

Above all, recognizing support staff for their unique and valuable contributions to student success is crucial. If a leader walks through their building or district and does not know their support staff's names, their roles, and their impact, something is wrong. These are the staff members in the trenches each day driving the bus, answering the phone, and working one-on-one with the most fragile students. A leader ignores their impact at great risk to their perceived and actual effectiveness.

Leaders should ask themselves, "do I know my support staff's names and their stories, and do I take every opportunity to recognize their impact and value?"

Chapter 13

Not Holding People Accountable

Holding people accountable is one of the most challenging dynamics when leaders transition from individual contributors to the system to being responsible for the system itself. As individual contributors, those staff members who fail to meet contractual obligations or otherwise act as cultural drains on the organization fall outside areas of responsibility. As a leader, however, effectiveness can often be measured by what is tolerated as behavior.

Most leaders succeed with holding people accountable when the transgressions are egregious or occur in public. Staff members who report to work intoxicated or under the influence of drugs, for example, are held accountable at high levels. These instances often go right up the chain of command to district offices and involve those at the cabinet level. The little, seemingly insignificant problems, however, are the ones that even effective leaders may not be comfortable confronting at times.

At first glance, some of these smaller items may not seem that significant on the surface. Some of the more common events that leaders may encounter could be:

- Staff members spend time grading papers in the back of the faculty meeting rather than participating in the meeting itself.
- Employees are five minutes late to open their classrooms consistently, leading to several students milling around the halls and requiring other staff members to provide on-the-spot and unscheduled supervision.
- Teachers who follow their own scope and sequence after participating in professional learning community time where the team agreed upon unit pacing and assessment timing.

In all three instances, the building and organization may continue to operate even though these incidents occur. None of them are so detrimental to the overall teaching and learning for all staff and students to merit cabinet-level intervention. All of them in their own way, however, reinforce among other staff that such behavior is going to be tolerated and thus quickly erodes culture within the building.

Failing to hold people accountable with these small items also leads to cynicism among highly-effective employees. For staff who participate in meetings, show up on time, and follow agreed upon team expectations, such transgressions slowly eat away at the camaraderie that is required to achieve group success. This is especially true if the leader knows about the behavior and fails to respond. In those cases, the leader's credibility takes a hit. Highly-effective employees want to work for highly effective leaders, and such leaders do not neglect addressing these types of issues.

There are many reasons why even good leaders fail to hold people accountable on these types of items. One reason is the normal human desire to be liked by everyone. Some leaders associate empathy with trying to understand everyone's perspective and make it okay for them to continue behaving in certain ways. Trying to be nice towards everyone often contributes to failing to hold people accountable.

In reality, letting people get by with subpar performance is the opposite of being nice. It is possible the employee does not realize the significance of being five minutes late and how that impacts their colleagues as they are trying to start their day. Moreover, the person may not understand that sitting in the back of the meeting grading papers sends a negative message to their colleagues. Helping employees realize the consequence of their actions is actually being nice; conversely, letting people slide by and drag down the organization is a very cruel way to lead.

Another reason leaders may develop bad habits in this area is that their own personal behavior is subpar. Is the leader also late to the building at times? Are faculty meetings hastily thrown together and essentially meaningless discussions? We all have an internal mechanism that lets us know when we are putting forth maximum effort. For leaders who are not putting this forth, they may find it hard to hold others accountable when they are not holding themselves accountable.

Finally, a major reason even good leaders may fail to hold people accountable is that they feel badly doing it. They know the person is going to be upset, and therefore the conversation is put off. Learning to not own other's emotions is a challenging leadership task. It takes time for many leaders to realize that someone else's reaction to your discussion is not on the leader; there is something in the other person that is causing them to react in a certain way.

For example, if a leader decides to confront the employee who is five minutes late and the employee blows up, the leader cannot own that reaction. Rather, there is something within the employee who understands their behavior is poor and their anger is their defense mechanism.

Thankfully, there are strategies leaders can employ to begin holding people accountable more effectively. First, leaders should be clear about expectations. This is especially true when hiring and onboarding new employees. The time to reinforce the importance of punctuality is at the beginning. If the entire grade-levels decision on scope and sequence is expected to be followed, leaders should be clear about that up front. Clear expectations at the get-go are critical to this process.

Furthermore, leaders should investigate the root cause of why people are acting in a certain way. Is it a lack of training? Is the building or organization a bad fit for the person? Moreover, there are times when leaders may not have the right people in the right seat on the bus. If a playground monitor has physical mobility issues, that particular setting may not be the right fit for that person. Getting to the root cause is important.

Finally, when the accountability conversation has been had, the emotions are out, and the root cause is identified, leaders should always offer people the opportunity to improve. There are certainly some cases and incidents where this may not be feasible. For most cases, however, setting an action plan and following up with support may help the employee turn their ship around. Always remember that the organization hired this person for a reason; there was something in their resume, their skill set, or their experience that would add value to the building. Offering people the chance to improve after holding them accountable is often the right thing to do.

By not holding people accountable for seemingly small transgressions, leaders can quickly erode goodwill and trust built among a staff. Tolerating subpar behavior is a poor way to lead. In taking stock of their staff behaviors, leaders should reflect upon what behaviors are allowed to be tolerated because they are "not really all that bad." Then, they should ask themselves, "by tolerating this behavior, what cost is there to building culture and trust?"

Chapter 14

An Overwhelming Need to Be "Me"

Leadership theories abound with the need for leaders to bring their authentic selves to their work. Leaders who do bring their whole selves to their work—their humility, their vulnerability—are more likely to realize that no one person can lead a building or organization alone. Schools, like all organizations, rely on staff to recognize that others can help make them better. Leaders can certainly model this ethic when they bring their authentic selves to the building.

This belief can veer into negative territory, however, when it becomes an overwhelming need to be "me." Everyone carries unique traits, talents, and competencies that translate to the workplace in a non-neutral manner. Aspects of our personality and personal practices can help move our work forward or hinder from that effort. This is especially true for leaders, who are uniquely positioned to impact culture on a larger scale.

For example, someone may relish the role of playing "devil's advocate" and questioning what they perceive as questionable thinking. While this may be part of a dinner-time conversation in some households, such a need to "be me" in the workplace may alienate colleagues and supervisors. Raising counterintuitive points to push a group's thinking is positive; questioning everything for the sake of being the "devil's advocate" quickly wears out one's welcome.

As aforementioned, the overwhelming need to be oneself within a team construct is one thing. Often, the group or team has other individuals within it that can offset this type of behavior. When the leader possesses this type of attitude, however, it has the potential to pull down the entire organization. There are several items that fall into this negative grouping, including:

- Gossiping. We have all been around leaders who love to pull others aside and try to get the scoop on someone else's struggles.

- Having "high standards." Of course, having high standards is a positive, but when standards are so high that a leader cannot praise others, there is a problem.
- Always needing to speak one's mind. Everyone's opinion has value, but not everyone's opinion has the same value on every possible topic.

Marshall Goldsmith writes about this habit in his bestseller *What got you here won't get you there.*[1] Goldsmith attributes this bad habit to what he calls a "pile of behaviors" that individuals use to define themselves. We may think "I am always on time" or "I always get back to people right away" and these thoughts may drive how our behaviors impact others. While these traits are personally positive, they may be projected on others in a less-than-positive manner.

For example, for a leader who self-identifies as "always on time," punctuality to meetings may be a high value. That is more than fine. It can veer into the negative, however, when the leader uses that personal trait to inform their leadership. There are times when people are going to be late to events. Especially with teachers with young children, the clock can sometimes be more of a guide than an absolute truth. If a leader values punctuality so much that they cannot be flexible when situations arise, their leadership effectiveness will suffer.

Moreover, a leader who values "getting back to people right away" may overemphasize the need to respond to emails. Being prompt in answering questions is a positive leadership trait; after all, it is all about service to others. Overvaluing "inbox zero," however, at the detriment of being visible and present in the school building, is a danger. If a leader is so focused on answering emails that they cannot spend time in classrooms and with staff personally, their leadership may suffer.

This overwhelming need to be "me" is most dangerous when it fosters a resistance to change and growth. Chances are the "way we are" has led to personal and professional rewards in lives and careers. This is especially true when the traits are perceived as positive in nature. Being prompt with replies was likely valued by a building principal when, as a teacher, the individual was asked to provide input into an initiative. This promptness may have led to an impression by supervisors that the teacher was responsible, on-the-ball, and could be trusted with more responsibility. These are all dynamics that can lead to an initial administrative position or at least positive references.

Stepping into a leadership role, however, that same trait can hinder effectiveness. As aforementioned, valuing quick email responses over getting out and about the building can lead to administrators spending far too much time at their office. What worked as an individual contributor to a larger system no longer works when the leader is now overseeing the system. There is too much to do and too many people to interact with to lead in such a manner.

If the leader holds this value too dear, they will be resistant to change. Every step in the journey requires a fresh set of eyes on our personal and professional practices. It is no different than graduating from high school and going to college; the habits that led to high school success may not lead to college success. Time management is harder; relationships may not be as solid. As with that major life change, every new rung on the career ladder requires the leader to spend time reflecting on their personal and professional practices.

One of the hardest transitions is going from individual contributor of a system to the leader of a system. All of a sudden, the leader is now responsible for far more moving parts than they were as a teacher or in a similar school role. Upon earning the first administrative position is a perfect time for leaders to start this level of reflection. Going up the ladder, however, requires a similar process. Leading as a building principal is different from leading as a Director or Assistant Superintendent.

At all stages of the game, leaders should ask themselves "are there situations where I find myself feeling like I need to be 'me?'" If the answer is yes, the leader should spend some time reflecting on their personal and professional practices and evaluating their impact on their leadership effectiveness.

NOTE

1. Goldsmith, Marshall, and Mark Reiter. *What Got You Here Won't Get You There: How Successful People Become Even More Successful*. 2007. Print.

Chapter 15

Not Being Solid with Your Family

Taking on a leadership role entails more work than being an individual contributor in the system. This is often true when accepting positions with increasing levels of responsibility. Building leadership roles undoubtedly require a great investment of time; work at the district level is typically more complex and involves leading several disparate groups. Both the time investment and increasing complexity of work often impact family life.

Leadership work impacts family life in other ways, as well. First, transitioning from a teacher role to an administrator role entails flexible hours. While teacher contracts usually contain clauses around start times, end times, lunch times, and prep times, administrative work does not involve those boundaries. Of course, many teachers work through lunch, come in early, and stay late. The point here is that those options no longer exist when they are needed.

These considerations, among several others, should be considered before jumping into an administrative position. These are important conversations on two levels. First, it is better to wait for a leadership opportunity that affords necessary work-life balance than one that requires the scales tilt too far towards work. Moreover, applying for administrative positions is not a solo act, especially for leaders who have spouses and children. Reviewing job descriptions with family and the "hidden" elements such as travel time, evening and weekend expectations, and other points is also crucial.

Being "solid" with family means having these conversations and the trusting relationship with family members to discuss ongoing challenges. It is not pursuing the perfect work-life balance mix because such perfection does not exist. Many administrative positions ebb and flow with time commitments, stress levels, and task completion. Seeking out information on potential positions, researching district culture, and discussing these findings with spouses and family members helps build that trusting relationship around work obligations.

Different leadership positions entail different work rhythms. For example, summer is the busiest time of year for personnel leaders. Hiring and onboarding staff for the new school year, handling contractual questions around transfers, and related topics makes taking long vacation stretches very challenging. For building leaders, by contrast, the summer time may be the perfect time to get away with family for a week or two at a time. Understanding what types of roles suit particular stages of life is important.

Often, being career-oriented and climbing the ladder runs counter to our family needs. This includes situations where others tap leaders on the shoulder for promotions to higher levels of responsibility. It is always nice to be wanted, but it is more important to be solid enough with family to discuss the impact those promotions would have on home life. The challenge is not framing these as "either-or" conversations but rather approaching them as "not yet." Principals, Assistant Superintendents, Superintendents—these positions will always be in demand. Phases of life, however, go by quickly. It is better to stay in a lower level of responsibility if it means enjoying young children while they are young than jumping to a higher position and missing out on those times.

Being solid with your family also means recognizing the rhythms within the currently held position and how those timetables impact family life. Every position entails busier seasons than others. A building principal, for example, will be more pressed for time during state testing season than during early July. A district-office director may be busier during summer months providing professional learning opportunities than during June when buildings are winding down their school year. Recognizing and communicating these ebbs and flows is crucial.

Taking this one step further, engaging with family in calendar planning can help set realistic time expectations. For example, many Cabinet-level administrators will have at least one night per month for a Board of Education meeting. These are usually 13–15 hour days when all is said and done. Families should be aware that those nights are ones where plans at home will not be realized. Recognizing this, however, can help leaders plan other opportunities during that same week to engage with family.

Shared digital calendars are a unique way to engage in planning. Especially for busy families where children are involved in multiple activities, time is always a finite resource. Laying out monthly expectations on a calendar can help identify opportunities for quality family time and help families know that time is coming even though specific days and evenings can be overwhelming. Building a shared sense of quality time is important for busy leaders who will inevitably have outside expectations placed upon them.

Leaders are also uniquely positioned to model this for this staff. Prioritizing work-life balance is a strategy that can have positive impacts on school culture. For example, refraining from evening and weekend emails to staff signals that leaders recognize those times should be devoted to family time and personal wellness. One strategy is to draft and save emails on evenings and weekends but send them during working hours. Most email platforms allow for scheduled email sending, furthermore, so that leaders can draft an email, schedule it, and know it will be sent during a specified time.

Most staff, upon seeing any communication from their supervisor, will feel a natural pull towards reading and reacting. Giving staff the grace to refresh and prioritize their own wellness beyond work hours will be recognized and appreciated. When leaders refrain from constantly bombarding staff with communication at all hours, staff realize that their administrator values them as whole persons. This necessarily can trickle down, as well, to how staff treat their students.

Overall, being solid with your family means open communication about work opportunities and rhythms and modeling this for all stakeholders. It is a mindset and approach to balancing leadership with personal and family life—both are important facets of life, but only when they work in tandem do leaders find professional and personal fulfillment. Leaders should reflect upon their communication patterns with family, staff, and self. Does the family know that this busy season will end and time can be repaid and reinvested? If not, engaging in some of these strategies may help leaders find some semblance of work-life balance.

Chapter 16

Talking Way Too Much

When thinking of leadership characteristics, too often those surrounding the leader as "hero" come to mind. Leaders always have to have the best ideas, find the right answers, and give inspirational speeches. While this may be true at times, leaders also may drift into bad habits around talking too much. At the end of the day, leadership is about empowering others to develop their own skill sets rather than top-down approaches emanating from the principal's office.

Many leaders are conditioned to associate leadership with talking too much early in their careers. In college, graduate school, and administrative preparation programs, class discussions are essential. Those who always speak up and lead those class discussions may be perceived as stronger than those who only interject every once in a while. Charisma tends to stand out, and leaders who may be more introverted may feel that they are missing a key leadership characteristic.

In reality, the opposite is often true. While charisma and leading from the front does come into play at times, it also tends to burn out others if practiced all the time. During a crisis or an emergency, leaders need to take charge. But when implementing a new program or initiative, gathering feedback and empowering others is a more sustainable leadership practice.

This is not to say that leaders should never talk too much. Rather, if leaders practice too much talking and gain a reputation for chatting people's ears off, their staff will begin taking small steps towards tuning them out. Often, this is a small leadership practice that surfaces over time. We have all worked for leaders who, when encountered in the main office or mail room, will talk throughout a teacher's entire prep period. Or, if they are encountered on the way into the building, will eat up valuable morning time with topics that are not time-sensitive.

How can leaders find the balance between promulgating their ideas, equipping staff with solid information, yet respecting their time? The first step is to be self-aware. For a week, take an inventory of this practice. This does not include when staff approach the leader, but rather when the leader is approaching staff. What is the topic being discussed? Is it chit-chat, or is it purposeful?

Being self-aware of time taken is one area. Another is being aware of conversation patterns. Many leaders, especially early in their careers, feel the need to expound upon their own history and experience to prove themselves to staff. This can lead to too many autobiographical conversations that eat up staff's time. Of course, most staff want to know who their leader is and what they stand for. They may not need to know about their new principal's high school baseball career, however.

Beyond autobiographical history, some leaders feel the need to always demonstrate their knowledge and add value to every conversation. Sometimes, a simple "thank you" or "let me get back to you on that" will suffice. Too much explanation or too much expounding upon knowledge reinforces the perception of talking too much.

Finally, some leaders feel pressure to always have a response in a conversation. Rather than listening to understanding, they are listening to respond. While the other person is talking, they are framing their response in their head. This is another area where leaders may practice more self-awareness. Being cognizant of what one's own mind is doing while the other person is talking is a useful skill.

Since leaders do have to talk, and talk a lot, how can they make sure they are not talking too much? First, leaders should be aware of times when their staff may wish to be approached, and times where staff need to get their own work done. Greeting staff in the morning as they check their mail is good, but following them down the hallway to talk about the disciplinary incident the day before may be too much. Schedule a meeting to discuss that rather than eat into the staff member's morning time to prepare for the day.

Additionally, nothing bothers teachers more than leaders who interrupt their instruction to deliver a message. Every now and again something is urgent; we all understand that. But leaders who consistently enter classrooms while students are learning, make it all about themselves, then leave and force the teacher to regroup their lesson will quickly be resented. Visiting classrooms to see students is great, but interrupting a teacher's hard-planned lesson structure is not.

Making use of planned meetings is another way to encourage feedback loops without talking too much. Whether during faculty meetings, professional learning communities, or other scheduled meeting times, leaders can move beyond a one-directional information flow and make it a two-way street. Staff can read announcements and reminders and ask questions; meeting time does not need to be dedicated solely to reviewing the school calendar.

Leaders can also practice building in some simple questions into their conversational patterns. We all know leaders who, once they get talking, keep talking without ever asking a question. After delivering information to a staff member, asking a simple "what do you think?" can be a powerful tool. Being self-aware of this practice is also necessary to truly engage staff in a two-way conversation.

Finally, leaders can go beyond the open door policy. On the surface, having an open door where students, staff, and stakeholders can access the leader and ask any question at any time sounds good. In practice, however, it represents a chaotic way to lead. Being accessible is a key leadership quality. Being accessible in an organized way is even better.

To be better organized, leaders should invest in feedback loops. The question raised at the faculty meeting should be sought out and answered either at the next meeting or sooner. Attending grade-level meetings and engaging staff at times that work for them builds trust. Empowering staff to work on their own solutions and seek feedback is powerful.

Additionally, leaders can leverage technology to establish feedback loops. Shared documents and survey tools can quickly gather feedback and help leaders follow-up on building and organizational issues. They also empower staff to provide more thoughtful feedback than on-the-fly during a hallway conversation.

Listening is perhaps the most underrated leadership tool. In this way, introverted leaders have an advantage over those who tend to lead with charisma or personality. Being able to step back, listen, and provide thoughtful feedback is powerful. Leaders who talk too much eat into staff time and staff may begin to actively avoid them in order to not "get caught." Breaking off a conversation with one's supervisor is awkward.

Leaders who have developed a habit of talking too much may not realize it. It usually is not the type of indiscretion that leads to poor test scores or toxic school culture. Staff may very much like their leader even if they talk too much. Leaders should ask themselves, however, when they are engaging staff in conversations and if there are ways to be more measured in this area.

Chapter 17

Managing Too Much Minutiae

There are always too many tasks, and too little time. All leadership positions come with responsibilities large and small, from managing large missions and vision to ensuring that small, mundane tasks are completed effectively and efficiently. It can be easy to fall into habits where focus rests on what is in front of us at the moment. When this happens, the unceasingly, endless tasks that have to be completed—minutiae—can interfere with larger-scale and higher-leverage leadership tasks.

The problem with this habit is not that the minutiae should be ignored; rather, it is that when leaders manage too much of the minutiae themselves they distract from their larger leadership vision. There are specific touchpoints in a career when leaders can fall into the bad habit of taking on too much of the minutiae themselves to the detriment of their overall effectiveness.

One primary time and place this can happen is when turnover occurs among staff. Preferably, staff turnover is predictable with retirement dates and other longer-runways to onboard new employees. Often, however, events occur where very little time—if any at all—exists to train successors to key positions. Leaders in a one-to-one relationship with staff members are most susceptible to this. In these scenarios, such as building principal and main office staff, tasks remain to be completed even though the support staff has departed.

In these scenarios, it is often necessary for leaders to step in and fill the gaps. Stepping up is an essential leadership attribute during these moments. Welcome-back letters still must be mailed. Report cards still must be stuffed. Computer lab schedules are always in a state of flux. These are tasks that would often be completed by main office staff. Critically important, yes, but minutiae managing at its best. The leader may have to step in and fill these gaps, and the key is to understand when it is time to step back out.

While the leader is filling the gap, they often discover ways to make tasks more efficient or change systems in some way. That is the benefit leaders have with this scenario. For a brief period of time, they can use their expertise with these tasks and better understand their support staff's duties and responsibilities. The challenge, however, is when leaders begin to own them and do not give them back. One mantra often heard is "it is easier when it just gets done." While that is true in the short-run, that time spent on managing the minutiae adds up to lost leadership in other higher-leverage areas.

When leaders step back and reflect upon all of the inputs that hit them on a daily basis, there are some important clues that may indicate they are managing too much minutiae. First, staff will often skip over steps in the chain of command because they know the leader will get them an answer right away. If a department chair is the point person for scheduling questions, and the principal receives and responds to questions before the department chair is involved, staff are signaled that they can go right to the top.

Being responsive to staff needs and questions is obviously an essential leadership quality. Enabling the chain of command to be passed over entirely, however, only adds to the leader's email inbox, line at the door, or list of phone calls to return. Reinforcing the process in a respectful and straightforward manner is also an essential leadership quality. If this latter quality is not exercised appropriately, the minutiae will continue to pile up.

Another reflection point for leaders is to step back and think about the direct systems they manage. Is the building principal the one teachers have to see to ask questions about the computer lab schedule? Or, can that be managed by someone else? It is important to have a clear schedule for staff to follow, but when the leader manages that level of minutiae, they are taking time away from other tasks.

The mistake in managing too much minutiae is a strategic one. When too much time is spent on important, yet low-leverage tasks, leaders are distracted from the larger work. There is comfort in the minutiae that often pulls leaders in. Completing these tasks provides a sense of finite completion—the letters have gone out and the completion is visible. The higher-leverage and larger work, by contrast, is often messier and less linear.

For example, if leaders can delegate their calendar to their office staff rather than schedule meetings on their own, they free up time to be around the building and district visiting classrooms and engaging in meaningful dialogue with staff. Putting a meeting on the calendar has a finite sense of completion while engaging with staff often leads to messy questions and items for follow-up. The latter, messier work, however, is where the long-term success lies. Every opportunity a leader has to delegate the lower-level tasks and engage in the higher-level tasks is one they should pursue.

What constitutes a higher-level task? They are usually less finite with ambiguous short-term outcomes. Principals who visit classrooms each morning to greet students usually do not have an immediate outcome in mind. Rather, the goal is to greet students, make them feel comfortable, and engage with staff. That process repeated consistently, however, builds trust among students and staff and leads to greater engagement down the road. It is not necessarily a measurable goal, but one that has hard-to-see longer-term benefits.

Leaders should be on the lookout for times when they may be managing too much minutiae. It happens easily and can creep up without notice. It can happen at various times and places such as when staff turnover occurs or when leaders have to step in and fill gaps for other reasons. Always recognizing the time trade-off is key. Time is the ultimate finite resource and how leaders choose to spend their time is a direct reflection on how they view their role. While bad habits can occur, being reflective is important.

If leaders find themselves managing too much minutiae, they should ask themselves "what is lost when I take too much on?" and "are there others in the organization who are able to help me with this?" Shifting from lower-to-higher level tasks is one key way to boost leadership effectiveness.

Chapter 18

Unprofessional Dress Habits

When you first enter a room or a meeting, you have one free moment—often an instant—where you have everyone's undivided attention. In that moment, people often decide in a split-second whether they find you credible or not as a leader. Especially working in school settings, where different norms about dress often reinforce the power of relationships, appearance and growing take on increased importance.

This chapter is not specifically about "how" a leader should dress, only that dress habits are important for leaders to consider. Often, a particular setting, cultural practices, and historical norms dictate what is and is not "professional" in a school. The point here is that dress habits matter and can often leave those around you with a slightly better or slightly worse impression of a leader's effectiveness. Fischel and Valentine[1] in 1984 began to explore issues around principal dress and surveyed staff in various school settings about their impressions. While their findings on three-piece suits and gray herringbone jackets may or may not be suitable today, their conclusions are relevant. They state that "the principal sets the direction taken by the school, or some would say, the 'tone' or 'climate' of the school.[2] Although one of many factors, leadership dress habits can contribute to or detract from a leader's perceived effectiveness.

Often, a leader's entry point into school administration can impact their dress habits. Many administrators who enter into school leadership maintain that, being a younger school leader, formal dress habits are important. For school leaders ascending to principalships and other leadership positions in their 30's, perceived readiness may be impacted by professional dress habits. One leader interviewed for this study stated:

When I first took a director position in a new district, I was walking around the high school on the first day of school. I didn't really know where different rooms were, so I understandably looked lost. One staff member asked if I was a student teacher and if I knew where the main office was. I later learned it was someone I would be conducting a formal observation of that year.

This school leader reflected that he maintained his formal dress habits but probably did look like a brand new student teacher on that day. It also reinforced with this leader how important dress was; imagine what would have been asked if he had on a polo shirt and jeans.

As leaders persist in their positions and build trusting relationships, their staff will get to know them more and more. When that happens, professional dress habits may be more relaxed. But initial first impressions are very important to a school leader's success. Some staff will have been involved in the formal interview process and will have that structured, more formal first impression. For most staff members, however, the first day of school may be the first introduction. Keeping that energy requires consistency with dress habits. Professional dress also helps a leader maintain confidence, promotes respect from others, and projects self-respect.

More importantly, however, in a school leadership role the principal often represents the school district in their public-facing interactions. When an angry parent calls and wants to meet with the principal, the principal IS the school at that moment. The principal's dress habits may influence how that parent interprets the school's response, speaks about the district in public to other parents, and even votes on the school budget.

Fair or not, a school leader will be evaluated each day by many people who will never see that leader's home or family. The vast majority of stakeholders and colleagues will never know the school leader personally, but they will interact with that leader professionally dozens of times throughout the day. From one-on-one meetings to large-scale parent nights, a leader's professional dress habits can positively influence how acquaintances rate and reflect upon a leader's effectiveness.

Some occasions may call for a relaxed dress code. An elementary principal in a school parade, for example, may don a silly costume in the name of school spirit. Holiday-themed ties and other school-themed articles may also be acceptable at different points in the school year. By and large, however, a school leader's work is going to be serious every day; there are rarely days off from that fact. A leader's appearance from greeting students off the bus, to the parent-teacher conference night presentation, to a moving up ceremony can all add to or subtract from stakeholder's perception of effectiveness.

Developing better habits around professional dress can take many forms, but several action steps are small and attainable. These would include:

- Planning for a few days ahead on Sunday evening. If not laying clothes out or organizing them in a closet, at least making a mental plan of what events are on your calendar and what dress is appropriate (i.e., a Summer Friday in the office may call for a Polo Shirt, but a Board of Education presentation likely calls for more formal attire).

- Doing any ironing on the weekends. Realizing that ironing needs to be done at 8pm the night before work may feel daunting. Rather, knocking this off your to-do list on the weekend while watching a favorite program may feel more attainable.
- Conducting a "wardrobe inventory" every three to four months. Which items are getting worn out? Doing this on a regular basis can prevent the sudden, once-a-year feeling that you "don't have anything to wear."

All in all, a leader's dress habits can help make or break their success. While not modeling for GQ, it is important that leaders reflect upon how they are presenting themselves to their stakeholders and colleagues on a daily basis and ask "is this helping or hurting my effectiveness as a leader?"

NOTES

1. Fischel, Frank, and Jerry Valentine. 1984. "Teacher Perceptions of Principal Dress." *The Clearing House* 58, no. 2 (October): 60–62. 104.225.168.145.
2. Ibid.

Chapter 19

Accepting Silence as Agreement

It can be easy to get faked-out by conversations and meetings that end in silence. For leaders, it is tempting to equate silence with agreement. This is particularly true after difficult meetings where challenging conversations are had. When difficult conversations are met with silence—and perhaps even feigned consent—the meeting may end amicably but the challenges are only beginning.

Most leaders, at some point in their careers, are uncomfortable in spaces and times where tension rises and does not easily dissipate. Moreover, most issues worth exploring in our schools require these environments. Any change effort worth implementing is going to make some staff get out of their comfort zones. When this happens, a continuum of responses exist. Some staff jump right on board. Others wait and see if the change is real. Others, of course, resist the change with every fiber of their being.

With all three groups, conversations also take various pathways. While some early adopters jump in right away, others need to process. Those in the middle may be most prone to respond with silence. This group is the most important because they likely represent the building or organization's critical mass. When this group exhibits silence rather than asking questions, challenging assumptions, or engaging further, leaders should take note. The final ground—the resistors—are going to resist, at least at first. While some will come around if the change effort is well-implemented, others may never do so.

Circling back to the critical mass, leaders need to pay the most attention to this group. When the majority of staff maintain silence, and perhaps nod and slightly smile, it can be tempting to associate this with agreement. This is the group where leaders should spend the time and energy exploring further conversations.

Getting comfortable with these often-uncomfortable follow-up takes time and experience. While some leaders may excel in this area right away, most need multiple at-bats in this area to gain proficiency. It is both a science and an art. Understanding what various feedback loops yield and when they fail to produce input represents the science side. Breaking down feedback loops and ensuring that they are functioning takes time.

Leaders also need to recognize and develop a "feel" for what their building and organization is experiencing. It is not enough to have strong systems in place for feedback. Leaders also need to develop their own situational awareness and develop a "sixth sense" for what staff are feeling. Developing this extra sense involves trust, time, and tension.

Any leader who has their building's pulse also possesses their staff's trust. Students, staff, and stakeholders are comfortable letting the leader know when change efforts are missing the mark or when decisions are not resonating. Building this trust helps the leader understand when and how to pivot. Taking this one step further, leaders who have this trust can also turn around and empower staff to be involved in the change efforts.

Additionally, developing this extra sense takes time. Being in and around the building, in classrooms, in the cafeteria, on buses, and other areas is essential. This cannot be developed by leaders being in their offices. Thankfully, leaders can stay connected to their main offices while also being around the building. Portable desks, smartphones, and other items can help leaders be connected to their hubs while also being physically present. The more leaders see and hear, the better sense they will have of these dynamics.

Finally, developing this sense requires tension. This may be counterintuitive, but strong organizations are ones that challenge the status quo. When leaders believe they have "the" answer, staff should be comfortable pushing back. An idea that runs the gauntlet of criticism and feedback is a better idea than one developed in a vacuum. There should be moments where staff are involved in vetting these efforts. While it may be uncomfortable, staff members who see items from different vantage points contribute significantly to these efforts.

To create this tension, leaders should create environments where students, staff, and stakeholders are comfortable challenging each other's ideas. When professionals trust one another, they can be comfortable challenging each other's ideas. Leaders can facilitate this culture by modeling feedback, asking for improvement suggestions, and verbalizing that feedback is essential. Over time, these efforts can contribute to a school culture where ideas run through a feedback process before germinating into implementation.

Challenging this process is that such dynamics are often hidden from view. When leaders step into new situations, these cultural norms are not immediately visible. The items that are visible such as class sizes, prep times, building organization, and others often detract from this focus. Leaders need to take care of those items. When those items are in place, however, leaders should go one step further and begin cultivating the trust, time, and tension necessary to move beyond silence as acceptance.

Staff often settle on silence instead of feedback because they do not believe their input matters. Most teachers, over their careers, will work for several principals and district-level leaders. Some of them may welcome this feedback, and others may want silence instead of feedback. Leaders, like all professionals, run the gamut with these attributes. Leaders need to be incredibly intentional with their staff that they welcome their feedback.

Then they need to reiterate that. And then reiterate it again. And again. This message should permeate the culture so that staff can make a good impression of the message behind the leader's back. There is no such thing as over communicating in this area. If not, it is likely that staff will slip back to their previous norm and practice silence. Many staff may not have ever worked in an environment where their feedback is truly welcomed on all matters. This message needs to be hammered home time and again to avoid slipping back to a culture where silence remains the norm.

When leaders are not receiving candid and honest feedback and are met with silence most of the time, they should ask whether the trust, time, and tension necessary has been invested. Most leaders will have made gains in these areas. Cultivating tension may be the dynamic that requires the most intentionality to move forward.

Chapter 20

Being Consistently
Late to Meetings

Among our school system's most identifiable markers is time. Employee contracts have start and end times. Many schools operate on a bell schedule that denotes how much time students and staff possess to travel from class to class. School starts on specific days and ends on specific days per a particular state's regulations. Schooling maintains a specific and definable time structure that often dictates who meets with who, and when meetings are held.

Although as a concept, time may possess specific cultural and meanings, in the world of schooling it is one of our most important markers. Research has demonstrated that an individual's relationship with time and lateness may impact their perceived effectiveness on the job.[1] Furthermore, lateness in meetings has been shown to negatively affect problem-solving abilities on both the individual and the team-level. This is especially true when it involves an employee being late for a meeting held by their supervisor. Research has demonstrated that when a higher status person is late for meetings, their lateness is often excused as being busy, while when a lower status employee is late, they are often viewed as possessing poor time management skills.[2]

In the professional world, everything that happens—or does not happen—has symbolic value. Whether part of a large administrative team or meeting one-on-one with an angry parent, the way leaders show up to meetings and their perceived level of preparedness matters greatly. Consider the difference between someone showing up for a meeting five minutes early with paper and pen in hand and someone showing up five minutes late, unprepared, and not entirely sure what the meeting is about. The meeting partner's perception of the leader's preparedness and credibility are dramatically different in those two circumstances.

This cuts to the chase as to why being on time and prepared for meetings is important, and why being consistently late for meetings is so deleterious. Being consistently late and unprepared for meetings erodes a leader's credibility. And any erosion of credibility in one area necessarily impacts the perception of credibility in other areas. If a parent is meeting with a Principal, who is always late for meetings, scattered, and unprepared to discuss the issues at hand, how can their word be trusted when they assure the parent that a problem will be addressed? Most stakeholders will never know their school leader on a personal basis; the leader's credibility, therefore, is one of their most valuable assets and must be protected and reinforced at all times.

Not only does lateness to meetings anger co-workers, it sets a negative impression of a leader's ability with their supervisors. For school leaders who are ready to seek the next step in their career, their credibility is crucial with their supervisors. If a building principal cannot show up to a meeting on time, how are they to be trusted with millions of taxpayer dollars, for example? Being consistently late for meetings is one of the little habits that can slowly but surely eat away at a leader's credibility and their chances for promotion.

It is inevitable that even the most punctual school leader will be late to meetings or other events at some point. Particularly for building leaders, the job is unpredictable and one event on a morning school bus, for example, can scuttle the entire morning's plans. In those cases, having the reputation for being on time and prepared is important. If a leader is already known as someone who respects others' time, they are usually given the grace by their colleagues and supervisors. A one-time event does not harm credibility; consistently, long-term trends do.

Leaders who know they are going to be late for meetings can implement some strategies to help. First, whenever possible, a school leader can have their office staff call their supervisor's office and let them know they are going to be late. Not only does a supervisor appreciate the head's up and respect for their meeting, but they can also start the meeting on time for others knowing that there's an explanation. It is also powerful with colleagues when a supervisor communicates that a fellow leader called ahead of time to inform her or him that something came up and they will be late. It sets a good model for the rest of the team.

Every now and again, a leader may also just lose track of time. It happens to the best of leaders on occasion. When that happens, the best route is to be honest and apologize. Rather than explain away lateness by blaming others, taking ownership of a mistake is one of the true signs of effective leadership. Just as being consistently on time and prepared bolsters credibility, owing up to an occasional lapse in time management also builds credibility.

BEING LATE AS THE LEADER

As referenced above, research indicates that staff are often more understanding when a supervisor is late to start meetings due to perceived busyness. While this may be true in small increments, it should not become a leadership habit. Everyone on the team is busy; while some work may be more complex and layered than others, everyone has important tasks to complete and are trying to fit their workload into their work day. When a leader is consistently late, it may be perceived as a sign of disrespect towards others and their workloads.

On the employee side, it may be easier to call a supervisor's secretary—a single point of contact—to inform them that you are going to be late. That can be harder to accomplish if you're the supervisor and running a meeting with several employees as participants. At the very least, if possible, texting or emailing staff that the meeting may start late is a sign of respect. While not every staff member will see it, enough will where they can spread the word to their colleagues that the supervisor had enough respect for their time to inform them of the late meeting start.

What habits can leaders build to help break a pattern of lateness to meetings, particularly important ones? A few examples of positive habits in this area are:

- Set a clock or watch five to ten minutes ahead. That way, even if you are running behind, you are still more or less on time.
- Mind your schedule. Often, being late to meetings is a result of over-booking, or trying to be all things to all people at once. On days with important meetings, leave the 30-minute block immediately before the meeting opens so you have some buffer time before the meeting actually starts.
- Prepare! Before the day is complete, take a look at tomorrow's calendar and lay out materials that you may need for a meeting. Set aside a particular part of your desk, or another area such as a table, that is dedicated to those materials. That way, if you are pressed for time immediately before the meeting, you know exactly where the materials you need will be.
- Set reminders in your calendar or phone. A well-timed ding or buzz may alert you that the current task or meeting needs to wrap up as another is 15 minutes away. Set the time for at least 15 minutes, if possible, to provide some breathing room in between meetings to gather materials and gather yourself.

If you are consistently late for meetings, what message does that send to your colleagues and supervisors? What small habits could you put in place to break this lateness?

NOTES

1. Wendelin van Eerde & Sana Azar, 2020. *Too Late? What Do You Mean? Cultural Norms Regarding Lateness for Meetings and Appointments*. Cross-Cultural Research, Volume 54 (2–3), pp. 111–129. DOI: 10.1177/10693971/119866132.

2. Ibid., pp. 123.

Chapter 21

Transferring Ownership for Poor Outcomes

Being a school leader is similar to being a small town mayor. Everything and anything ultimately ends up under the leader's umbrella. From state account-ability data to lights in the school parking lot, leaders are responsible for being on top of outcomes big and small. Taking responsibility for all of these outcomes is one of leadership's greatest challenges.

Before moving into administrative positions, most school leaders operate within the system as contributors. Whether teachers, related support service providers, or other positions, these contributor positions are usually within the teacher's contract and contain closely monitored boundaries on time and responsibilities.

Start and end times, class size caps, and prep period language no longer exist when moving into administration. As an individual contributor to the system, these professionals maintain significant responsibility, but it is usu-ally guarded by boundaries. Individual classroom teachers, for example, are usually not responsible for whether their colleagues attend faculty meetings or dutifully fulfill their contractual obligations.

All of this changes upon entering administration. No longer an individual contributor to the system, leaders are now responsible for the system's opera-tion. Those professionals who are not fulfilling their contractual obligations are the leader's responsibility. Start and end times no longer exist. Assuming ownership for all outcomes, large and small, becomes paramount to success in these roles.

Part of this challenge rests with understanding perspectives on the profes-sion. Most leaders who take all of the classes, sit for the state-level exams, and apply for positions possess passion for the work at high levels. It is not that individual contributors to the system are not passionate; most are very passionate about student success. The difference rests in that possessing these high levels of passion is now the leader's job. Being successful in these roles requires that leaders possess the passion necessary to assume this level of ownership over outcomes big and small.

Even above-average leaders may fall into bad habits around transferring ownership for poor outcomes. This can show up in ways both big and small. Some of the small ways that even effective leaders may fall into the trap could sound like:

- "The unfortunate playground incident happened today because we were short monitors and there were not any substitutes available."
- "The classroom is at the entire other end of the building, and it can be very difficult to respond to emergencies in a timely manner."
- "If the district office gave us the resources we really need, then we could actually show improvements in test scores."

The reality is, when given the keys to the building or the district office (literally, given the keys to lock and unlock the door), the leader becomes responsible for everything that happens within that environment. Paradoxically, it is impossible for one person to be on top of every situation and be aware of every single blind spot that may exist. This is where systems and feedback loops come into play.

Leaders can demonstrate effective leadership through sheer will, charisma, and determination—up to a point. No one is talented enough, smart enough, for possessing enough foresight to see every angle. When leaders rely on their own individual talent to lead a school or organization, they often end up saying things like the three bullet points listed above. While these items may not rise to crisis-level, ownership for their outcomes are transferred to other dynamics at play.

Systems and feedback loops are the antidote to those three statements above. The statements may be factually correct, of course. The key to taking the next step is to add one more sentence that redistributes ownership to where it belongs and produces forward-thinking strategies. Revisiting those statements could look like this:

- "The unfortunate playground incident happened today because we were short monitors and there were not any substitutes available. *We need to create a rotation system for covering times when we need more playground supervision. Let's brainstorm ways we can do this at our next faculty meeting.*"
- "The classroom is at the entire other end of the building, and it can be very difficult to respond to emergencies in a timely manner. *In the future, let's take our laptops and phones and be active throughout the building*

when these triggers seem most likely to occur, and then we can start brainstorming how to prevent them."

- "If the district office gave us the resources we really need, then we could actually show improvements in test scores. *While we may not have every single item we think we need, let's look at the strengths we have and see how we can build upon them."*

Each statement's next sentence represents not only an action step, but the leader taking responsibility for creating better outcomes. It is not that the leader needs to solve every single problem, but they should take responsibility that the problems get solved.

Moving away from this mindset and beginning to take ownership for all outcomes has to involve leaders engaging students, staff, and stakeholders. Creating systems and feedback loops that involve anonymous surveys, brainstorming sessions, and other ways for teams to provide input is crucial. Solving some of these seemingly smaller items can lead to significant results.

Leaders should be attuned to the language they employ when something goes off the rails. Is ownership transferred to someone else? Or is language used that makes such an outcome seem inevitable? Some challenges are more easily solved than others, but very few items cannot be figured out at all. If leaders find themselves using language that transfers ownership for poor outcomes, they should think about ways to add that additional sentence that redistributes ownership back to them and points to a more hopeful future.

Chapter 22

Not Adapting Language
to Fit Your Audience

Education is a jargon-filled profession where insiders have access to information which outsiders do not. ESSA. FERPA. Common Core. And the list goes on and on.Leaders should avoid using inside language on outside audiences. Moreover, adapting language, tone, and word choice to meet one's audience is a trait that good leaders share. Failing to do so often breaks down trust and leaves outsider stakeholders feeling alienated from the process.

The process, of course, is educating other people's children. It is critical, therefore, that leaders adapt language to build trust rather than create barriers. When discussing a bullying situation, it is far better to address the situation from the parent perspective than explain the anti-bullying law's fine points. Most parents are not concerned that the law provides a 36-hour window to contact families, for example. Rather, they want to know that the school leader cared enough to contact them as soon as possible. Leaders who view language adaptation as a trust-building experience are more likely to develop strong relationships.

Adapting language to fit the audience is essential to effective leadership, especially in crisis situations or when emotions run high. When an angry parents calls the school, there are several items about which they may not want to hear:

- Board Policy: framing a decision around policy is always a strong decision, but citing policy verse by verse depersonalizes the conversation.
- Federal and State laws: using acronyms may only confuse outside stakeholders and can raise emotions even higher.
- Generalizing the situation: parents and stakeholders want to hear about their child's safety and well-being, not what is being done in relation to other students.

All three points above are important and may arise during a conversation. The key here is not "leading" with those points, but rather starting off with the shared commitment to the student's safety and well-being.

Remaining focused on the student keeps the conversation grounded in shared purpose.It also keeps the focal point on the student, which is why the conversation is happening in the first place. When leaders put themselves in the stakeholder's shoes and approach conversation from their perspective, they are less likely to use bureaucratic language.

Tailoring communication styles to match an audience is a sign of respect. Other parties can recognize when leaders are listening simply to respond as quickly as possible. Conversely, when leaders listen to understand rather than listen to respond, active listening occurs and fosters a deeper conversation. Adapting language to fit one's audience necessitates humility and vulnerability because it assumes that the leader may not have the "right" answer. Only through give and take, back and form, conversation with the other person or party does the appropriate response evolve.

Recognizing that language needs to be adapted is the key first step. This is especially critical when leaders communicate with diverse audiences. Key phrases and lingo that translate to those like ourselves may not resonate with those who have different life experiences.

Assuming, for example, that all parents have had positive school experiences can lead conversations astray. Often, parents are upset with the school system's handling of their child's situation because they too experienced similar trauma. Most school leaders likely had positive school experiences that influenced their decision to work in schools. Not everyone shares that perspective.Self-awareness that others may not share the same vantage point is critical.

A leader's race, ethnicity, socioeconomic status, sexual orientation, and other dynamics may influence their communication patterns. We cannot assume that others share our view of the world.This misconception may create a disconnect between leaders and their audience and break down trust.

It is especially important to recognize that, as the school leader, everything is a reflection of one's leadership. For example, calling teams "blocks" may communicate to students with incarcerated parents that school is similar to a prison environment. While seemingly small in scope, these little communication patterns can either build or break trust with parents and stakeholders.

How, then, can leaders get outside their comfort zones and communicate effectively with their audiences? There are several ways that capacity may be built in this area:

- Hold community focus groups that discuss how the school interacts with various stakeholders.Some areas, such as the "block" example above, may surface in these environments.
- Make home visits.Leaders can glean a lot of information on their audience from making home visits or even walking around the neighbors that feed their schools.
- Reflect upon their own implicit biases.We all have them, and when leaders recognize their own implicit bias, they are better positioned to understand how others may interpret their actions and communication.

This last point is important. Adapting language to fit one's audience requires leaders to confront their own implicit biases. For example, assuming that families can all attend after-school programming without school-provided transportation is an example of implicit bias.Some parents lack cars; it has nothing to do with "caring." Believing that the parents who show up at Open House are the ones that "care enough" is an example of implicit bias.

From that example, it is easy to develop dozens of similar cases where implicit bias may negatively impact relationships. This is especially true with stakeholders who have different life experiences than most teachers and administrators. Failing to recognize these implicit biases and neglecting to adapt language accordingly is a surefire way for stakeholders to call the central office with a complaint.

Failing to adapt language to meet the audience is a poor leadership habit that should be corrected as soon as possible. While not every conversation will go smoothly all the time regardless, recognizing this habit will help build trusting relationships with stakeholders. Leaders should reflect on their communication style and ask themselves:

- Do I use a lot of insider jargon when talking with stakeholders?
- Do I keep the conversation focused on the student's safety and well-being?
- Am I reflective of my own implicit biases and how they may impact communication?

Chapter 23

Getting on the Wrong Side of Important Gatekeepers

For the most part, school systems are conventional organizations with layered hierarchies, past practices, and deep histories. While innovation has been a buzzword in education for over a decade, the fact remains that most American school systems operate under the same set of rules as they have for years. Students move grade-to-grade through school from Kindergarten to Grade 12. While some variation occurs, most schools parse elementary years, middle years, and high school years separately. The overall structure of schooling remains relatively unchanged in our recent history.

With that consistency comes the status quo; "the way things have been done around here." This is not all negative. Every successful organization has predictable patterns and culture. If new structures and configurations were implemented each year, students and staff would struggle to find consistency in practice. Despite different Superintendents, Boards of Education, Principals, and others, most districts consist of patterns that may be relatively unchanged over several years.

If the average Superintendent's tenure is less than five years, then how does the status quo maintain supremacy for so long? While many reasons exist, one major consideration is the role that important gatekeepers play in organizational consistency. Gatekeepers are staff members who are uniquely positioned to control access to leaders, access to information, and access to processes and systems. They are also key staff members for other employees to navigate if they wish to access any of those above-listed dynamics.

Leaders can get on the wrong side of important gatekeepers in several ways. It is important to recognize who these gatekeepers in a school system could be. Some examples of staff who sit in unique positions to impact access, information, and processes are:

- Secretary to the Superintendent and District Clerk.

- A building's head custodian.
- The district's business official (who may carry one of several various titles).
- A district's personnel department.

All of the above individuals and team members pay critical roles in a building and district's success. They also work on various items that are not directly accessible to staff members. The personnel department, for example, works in a highly bureaucratic area where access to state-level certification systems are off-limits to most individual teachers. Moreover, the district's business official can help make or break desired changes to a W-4. All of these positions control access to information and processes that everyday employees struggle to navigate without support.

Getting on the wrong side of such gatekeepers is a dangerous practice. It is not that individuals in such positions are inherently manipulative and will work against employee questions. Rather, chances are that those in such unique positions are just like all others in school systems in general; they are human beings who carry their own talents and challenges with them on a daily basis. Leaders should recognize that gatekeepers are human, like everyone else, and respond to the same positive approach as everyone else.

There are basic and straightforward steps that leaders can take to work collaboratively with important gatekeepers. First, being polite and demonstrating respect for the gatekeeper's position is vital. This does not mean sucking up to the individual or manipulating conversations. Chances are, the Superintendent's secretary has been in their position longer than the Superintendent, and may have seen several come and go. Respect for that experience should be paramount.

Moreover, practicing active listening skills can help move the needle. By listening for a gatekeeper's needs, leaders can better tailor their message for maximum impact. For example, contacting the Superintendent's secretary the day after a Board of Education meeting rather than the day before a meeting may give the message a better chance of reaching the Superintendent. Being attentive to the gatekeeper's needs is important. If the gatekeeper's interactions are similar to everyone else's, then they are likely hit with one-sided demands all day. Being the leader who listens, rather than demands, can be a tremendous advantage.

As a combination of the above two points, the most important item for leaders to consider when engaging gatekeepers is that they are likely to be hit from all sides, all day, with people wanting to charge past the gate. Head custodians, for example, receive calls from morning until night from staff members who need additional items in their classroom, request the temperature in the room changed, or have similar requests. It is natural for any human being to wear down at some point in the face of such demands. The leader who is considerate of a gatekeeper's workload and takes their perspective into account is more likely to be granted access past the gate than those who continue to take, take, and take.

Of course, the converse is also true. Leaders who present daily demands without being considerate of others' workloads are less likely to have their messages presented in a speedy manner. Those who fail to respect the gatekeeper's history, power, and position are less likely to broker relationships across the organization. Every email, every phone call, every face-to-face interaction is an opportunity to build this key relationship.

School systems, as mostly conventional organizations, are laden with hierarchies and power relationships. Those in gatekeeping positions are likely to have longevity with the organization and relationships across several different departments. They are the ones who know "how things actually work." Moreover, the basic structure and systems that exist in schools have remained relatively unchanged for decades. A gatekeeper's experience and relationships are key components in any school's day-to-day operations.

Leaders would do well to recognize these practical matters and use them to their advantage. Cultivating relationships with key gatekeepers is an essential means to getting business done. Head custodians can facilitate after-school programming set-ups. Business officials can process time sheets with payroll expeditiously. Personnel departments can facilitate help cut through red tape for certification questions. These—and many other—gatekeeping positions have access to systems, information, and processes that most regular employees do not. Leaders can help themselves and their staff by forming strong relationships with these gatekeepers.

Most importantly, leaders should reflect upon their relationships with those in such positions. Does the Superintendent receive messages sent over? Does the lobby floor have a new coat of wax when the building hosts a board meeting? Does the leader's staff see their overtime pay in the most recent paycheck, or do they have to wait until the next one? If the answer to these questions causes pause, then leaders should reflect upon their relationship with key gatekeepers and think through how to help it improve.

Chapter 24

Associating Mistakes with Failure Rather than Opportunity

When school leaders land their first administrative position, there is often pressure to prove to stakeholders their worth. This is especially true when leaders leave one school district for a promotion in a new school district. This need to "prove oneself" often leads to an overwhelming desire to avoid mistakes. Associating mistakes with failure rather than as a growth opportunity is fostered by such a mindset.

Most stakeholders, however, work for a leader who demonstrates humility and vulnerability rather than one who feels they must always be correct. Especially in education—where a leader is surrounded by professionals and experts in their craft at all times—leaders need not feel like they must possess every answer. Leaders who are adept at facilitating solutions through others rather than creating solutions on their own find the most success.

As mistakes are inevitable in any walk of life, especially leadership, the way in which leaders approach mistakes is crucial for their own development and their school's success. Rather than see mistakes as symbolic of talent level, mistakes should be perceived as opportunities to learn something new and grow as a leader. When this happens, leaders not only help solve immediate concerns, but develop systems that prevent the same mistake from occurring again.

Research has demonstrated that mindsets around mistakes and growth exist at the individual and cultural levels. Dweck[1] has written at length about fixed versus growth mindset. Clearly, a growth mindset is required to approach mistakes as opportunities rather than failures. Willingness to learn and grow, rather than innate talent, is what propels leaders to continually improve at their craft.

By leading from such a perspective, moreover, leaders can foster a mindset culture that extends to their entire school or organization. Murphy and Dweck[2] explored how a leader's mindset influences other's mindsets, as well.

While individuals can possess fixed or growth mindsets, cultures often mirror the leader's approach. The authors discuss "cultures of genius" versus "cultures of growth" that can either hinder or facilitate organizational learning.

In a culture of genius, fixed mindset assumptions lead to stakeholders to try to outperform others, rank and sort employees by perceived talent, and create competitive rather than collaborative structures. Conversely, in a culture of growth, individual talent comparisons are minimized and the focus rests on creating collaborative space for teams to solve problems together. The latter mindset not only often reflects the leader's mindset, but also creates spaces where all stakeholders work together in a learning mode to address problems.

To facilitate a culture of growth, some prerequisites are necessary. First, the leader must possess a growth mindset themselves and model the humility and vulnerability necessary to learn from mistakes. When leaders make mistakes in public and grow from them, stakeholders notice. When leaders model vulnerability and take public risks, it positively impacts the entire organization. It sends a message that it is okay to make mistakes; stakeholders learn that they will not be penalized for making mistakes because everyone is entitled to make mistakes and learn from them.

Additionally, this culture creates psychological safety necessary for others to follow suit. Edmondson[3] has demonstrated that when team members hold the shared belief that risk taking is safe, a culture of growth can thrive. Leaders can enable this culture to grow by modeling the humility and vulnerability necessary to learn from mistakes.

There are some realities that leaders should understand that may help them move towards the necessary humility and vulnerability to create such a culture. First, stakeholders would rather work for a humble leader who listens and facilitates rather than a know-it-all who thinks they have the answer to every problem.

The reality is that one person will never know enough, or have enough experience, to be smarter than the entire organization. The room is always the smartest person in the room. No principal, for example, is smarter than the collective experience of their entire faculty. Staff would rather work for a building leader who makes a mistake and owns it rather than someone who feels they must always be correct and cannot recognize their own faults.

Secondly, most leaders will never be expert enough in all areas to even think they have all of the answers. A high school principal, for example, is likely certified in one or two content areas. The entire building is composed of professionals with certifications in dozens of areas. The certified music teacher possesses skills and competencies that the expert chemistry teacher can learn from and vice versa. Facilitating growth in others, rather than playing the expert, is what grows a culture of growth.

Finally, making mistakes and learning from them makes leaders appear human and builds connections with stakeholders. While leaders do need to operate above the fray, stakeholders appreciate that they also possess the same vulnerabilities as everyone else. Making those human connections with staff builds trusting relationships and facilitates the sense of "being in this together." This is especially important at the district level where staff possess fewer opportunities to see the leader in action. Being real and being human goes a long way with staff and stakeholders.

When leaders associate mistakes with growth rather than with failure, they open up fresh possibilities for shared growth. Not only does the leader grow, but this approach also develops a culture of growth at the building and organizational levels. When leaders realize that their actions are contagious and modeling vulnerability helps the entire organization feel safe taking risks, a culture of growth can flourish. With risks, come mistakes. Seeing them as opportunities rather than failures is an essential part of this process.

When thinking through their approach to mistakes, leaders should ask themselves—"when making mistakes, do I view them as failures or as chances to model vulnerability and grow?" The answer to that question will be far-reaching for all stakeholders.

NOTES

1. Dweck, Carol S. 2006. *Mindset: The New Psychology of Success*. New York: Random House.

2. Murphy, Mary C., and Carol S. Dweck. "A Culture of Genius: How an Organization's Lay Theory Shapes People's Cognition, Affect, and Behavior." Personality and Social Psychology Bulletin 36, no. 3 (March 2010): 283–96. https://doi.org/10.1177/0146167209347380.

3. Edmondson, Amy. "Psychological Safety and Learning Behavior in Work Teams." Administrative Science Quarterly 44, no. 2 (June 1999): 350–83. https://doi.org/10.2307/2666999.

Chapter 25

Not Intentionally Planning and Scheduling

When leaders lack an intentional planning routine, it does not mean that they lack any planning at all. To be moderately successful in any leadership position, some semblance of future planning is needed. Building principals responsible for state testing security, for example, have to plan for test delivery, storage, security, administration, collection, and all other related facets. To fail in this regard would ensure years of test misadministration and likely work the school leader out of their current position over time.

This bad leadership habit revolves around a failure to give planning and scheduling its proper place in leadership effectiveness. Similar to the first-year teacher who has to be intentional with all aspects of instruction because everything is new, school administrators should approach all aspects of their practice with this regard. There are several reasons why some leaders fail to give planning and scheduling its proper due.

First, many leaders have risen through the ranks without having to intentionally plan. Either they were highly competent at lower positions and were able to succeed in spite of this bad habit. Those successful as assistant principals, for example, may not have been directly responsible for the more-complex building leadership responsibilities. Communicating with Parent-Teacher Associations, organizing teacher observation schedules, and being the point person for all parent phone calls require time and effort.

Moreover, many leaders may assume that leadership positions necessitate chaotic days and constantly being pulled in various directions. While organized chaos is always part of the deal, leaders may not realize that by structuring their day in specific ways or planning blocks of time intentionally, they can mitigate this madness. While some days are chaotic due to outside forces, not every day has to be this way. A few intentional scheduling habits can bring needed structure to any busy day.

Finally, another major reason some leaders develop bad habits around intentional planning and scheduling is because they have not developed positive habits in this area. As counterintuitive as that may sound, the bad habit in this case is not having a positive habit with which to replace it. Later in this chapter, a few intentional habits will be shared that can help leaders replace the lack of a planning habit with the beginnings of a system to help organize and structure their time more effectively.

Intentional scheduling is critically important as leaders move up the ladder in their careers. Complexity increases with each increased level of responsibility. While a teacher is responsible for their classroom, a principal is ultimately responsible for all classrooms, even if they are not directly involved. An incident in a classroom ultimately ends up in the principal's lap. Likewise, a district-level leader is responsible for classrooms across multiple buildings, grade-levels, and content areas. Each step up the ladder brings increased complexity, making the need for intentional planning all the more important.

When thinking about intentional planning and schedule, there are two areas around which leaders should focus: tasks and people. Every administrative position involves a series of tasks that just need to get done, and get done well. Testing schedules need to be written, teacher duty schedules developed, and faculty meetings planned. These are not unimportant tasks, but they often involve a leader needing time to think through logistics. Scheduled time to have that bandwidth is important to work through a task efficiently and effectively.

More importantly, there is intentional time to plan with people. This can look differently depending on the leadership role. A building leader, for example, may look to block off the first 30 minutes of each day visiting classrooms and greeting students. While incidents may arise that prevent this from happening daily, having that time intentionally planned in a calendar dramatically increases the likelihood it will happen.

Moreover, building leaders may wish to block out student lunch times to be present in the cafeteria and hallways. By not scheduling meetings during these times, building leaders may find they are more proactive in handling issues that arise during these less-structured student times, and increase the time they have to work on tasks in the afternoon before dismissal. In this way, investing in people's time increases the ability to invest in task time later on.

District-level leaders may wish to invest in people's time in a more structured manner. Often, district-level leaders sit in specific bureaucratic positions on the organizational chart; they report to a supervisor, yet have others who report directly to them. They may not be directly involved in some aspects of the work, but need to have a handle on several situations to provide guidance and support their teams.

Rather than being present when events are happening like lunch and recess, scheduling time in this manner for district-level leaders requires intentionally structuring one-on-one or team time with staff. By scheduling these more-frequent, intentional check-ins, questions can be answered and problems solved in a timely manner. Similar to building leaders, by scheduling this time with people, district-level leaders may be able to free up more bandwidth to tackle the multiple tasks that constantly need to be completed.

While there is not a single best way to engage in a planning and scheduling habit, there are some key directions. First, it needs to become something that happens every day with a specific tool. This tool should be an efficient way to track tasks that need to be done, important communication to send, and a way to track "what's next." Digital apps exist that can capture this information. All smartphones possess the capacity to capture voice memos, for example, and leaders can record a voice memo at the end of each day with the important tasks that need to be completed the next day.

Paper-based planners are also useful as long as they follow a similar format. Consistency is key. Along with consistency, keeping it simple is important. Scheduling more than one or two major tasks to complete on any given day is a recipe for burnout. On a daily basis, keeping it simple and consistent are two themes that are important with intentional planning and scheduling.

On the weekly and monthly level, leaders should get in the habit—at least once a week or once a month—of reviewing their past schedules and upcoming schedules and evaluating their time decisions. Were tasks completed on time? If not, why not? Was there intentional scheduling for people built into the schedule? If not, where can it be developed? Reflection is an important aspect to develop this habit.

Finally, there are critical parts of each day, week, and month that leaders should be attuned to. Scheduling heavy tasks for Monday morning, for example, should not be prioritized. Monday mornings are for people whenever possible; staff have had the weekend to think about all of their questions, students are coming back into a structured environment, and the leader's presence in and around the building sets the positive tone. This is especially true coming off of long school breaks.

Throughout all of this, it is important to keep intentional planning and scheduling in the right frame of mind. The goal is not to squeeze more tasks into one's workday. Rather, the desired outcome is more balance between people and tasks. And with more balance in that equation, leaders may find they have more time to balance between work and home. Consistently going home stressed out and not able to give oneself freely to their family is not worth the extra money and prestige that comes with any leadership position.

Leaders should reflect upon their planning habits—or lack thereof—and think about how they might build more intentional habits into their routine.

If leaders feel a constant tension between tasks and people and never have enough time for both, an honest look at their habits in this area may yield more balance.

Chapter 26

Tolerating Poor Organizational Culture

Organizational culture is a collection of values, expectations, and practices that guide and inform the actions of all team members. These are the traits that make an organization what it is. Often, they can be difficult to discern for outsiders but govern the day-to-day existence of those within the organization. Organizational culture is not the team's mission statement or goals, although they may inform those public pronouncements.

Organizational culture is exemplified by habits and expectations that exist among the team and they are often exercised from above. Leaders, therefore, possess incredible power to make or break organizational culture. Finally, organizational culture is usually perceived through a series of outcomes and processes. How many employees voluntarily leave the organization each year? Are there feedback mechanisms that allow employee voice to influence decision-making? What do most team members within the organization spend their time talking about?

The above three questions—and many, many more—are influenced by the leader's day-to-day practices. Leading by example, and misleading by example, are both ways in which leaders can influence organizational culture. However, leaders also need to get to the ground level and discern their organizational culture in buildings, classrooms, and in the community. Doing so requires that leaders not neglect fundamental feedback loops that can inform organizational culture.

There are telltale signs that leaders are tolerating poor organizational culture. These can include, but are not limited to:

- Leaders not knowing their employee's names, or being connected to classrooms and buildings. In large districts, it may not be possible to know every single person, but being in and around buildings will build familiarity.

- Observing many early-career employees leaving within their first five years. While some will relocate to other areas due to relationships, watching employees leave consistently for neighboring districts is a telltale sign that something is amiss.
- Formal and informal conversations are not focused on the organization's "core business." In schools, the core business is teaching and learning. While other issues will inevitably creep in, teaching and learning should be the district's lodestar.
- Consistently hiring from within or hiring primarily for "cultural fit." Every organization requires some "fresh eyes" to constantly push towards improvement. If everyone looks the same, thinks the same, and has the same institutional history, chances are that little will change.

Superintendents, principals, and other school leaders are uniquely positioned to move organizational culture forward or simply tolerate poor practices. Both are easy to do, and easy not to do. This is not to say that new leaders should immediately upend a district's entire organizational culture. Listening to all stakeholders and soliciting board feedback—particularly from those who are critical—is essential. By listening to broad stakeholder feedback, leaders can craft

Tolerating poor organizational culture can also occur at the highest levels. Because organizational culture often flows downhill—meaning, the leader may not perceive how positive or negative it is in the moment because they are not close enough to it—leaders can get faked out with poor cultural habits. They may not perceive how poor culture is until it is too late.

Beyond the outcomes listed above, there are other practices leaders may practice or encourage that contribute to poor organizational culture. Most employees want to please their supervisors and are reluctant to directly tell them that their practices are leading to poor organizational culture. While a trusted colleague may come along from time to time, often these practices can go unchecked for years because no one told the Superintendent, Principal, or other school leader how their practices impacted culture. Some of these practices that negatively impact culture can be:

- Being inconsistent with communication. While supervisors may tell their employees that they should not check email on vacation, they will then go ahead and send them emails on vacation. Yes, the employee can respond when they return, but emails from supervisors often trigger a "get it done now" mentality with employees who want to please.
- Micromanagement. There are times when leaders need to take a little more control, but most of the time leaders will empower their teams more by delegating and trusting rather than trying to dictate everything.

- Failing to recognize top performers and celebrate their accomplishments. While most great teachers and administrators do their work because they love making a difference, if their work consistently goes unnoticed, it can damage their long-term commitment.

Most importantly, leaders promote poor organizational culture when they fail to confront poor behavior. This does not mean behavior so egregious that it makes the front page of the paper or ends in the police blotter. Tolerating the borderline rude, inappropriate, and toxic behaviors that build up over time is a poor leadership habit.

There are many reasons why leaders fail to confront the more-minor toxic behaviors that can permeate an organization. First, they may not have all of the facts, and feel that they are singling out an employee for something that may not be their fault. If an employee is consistently late, for example, there may be several reasons why the behavior is occurring. Leaders may not feel comfortable diving into someone's personal life.

Moreover, the behavior may not be "that bad." Some behavior—as a one time occurrence-may not be that bad. However, practiced consistently over time, it can negatively impact morale on the whole team. If the building and district is committed to a program, for example, and a handful of teachers refuse to participate, the message is sent that the program does not really matter. While others may still carry forward, they implicitly know that those who refuse to participate face little repercussions. The next time the district wants to onboard a program, they will be a little less likely to dive in wholehearted.

Being accessible, creating feedback loops, and actively listening to all stakeholders are ways that leaders can avoid tolerating poor cultural practices. Leaders should ask themselves, are my actions—or inactions—contributing to poor organizational culture?

Chapter 27

Throwing Others Under the Bus

Accepting responsibility when things go awry is one of leadership's essential cornerstones. School leaders make hundreds, if not thousands, of decisions every day. Some of these decisions are small-scale in nature, such as whether to call for an indoor recess when outside temperatures are low. Others are larger in scale, such as whether to retain an employee or grant tenure to a teacher. Accepting responsibility for these decisions is a highly-rated leadership quality.

Some leaders struggle in this area and the impact on leadership effectiveness can be devastating. When leaders fail to take responsibility for their decisions, or throw others under the bus as a response, not only is school effectiveness decreased but trust can be broken. Most stakeholders understand that leaders are not going to be right all of the time; rather, they will give a trusted leader the space to make a wrong decision and own it.

Throwing others under the bus is a very poor leadership habit. Moreover, it is a habit that plays out in explicit and implicit ways. Most noticeably, leaders will vocalize their transfer of blame for decisions or rationalize them away in conversations with others. Some examples of this can be common throughout the course of a school day:

- "The head custodian gave me the wrong forecast, so of course students were outside when the rain storm hit."
- "The Central Office never gives me all of the needed staff and they are the reason why school safety is a concern."
- "Your scores could obviously be better if you had a more effective co-teacher in your classroom."

In each instance, the person being thrown under the bus is likely not part of this conversation. This goes beyond mere vent and spills over into gossip. One of the most untrustworthy habits for a leader to possess is to gossip with staff about other staff members. Once staff know that the leader will make such comments behind others backs, they instinctively know that the leader will comment about them, as well, when they are not present.

Deflecting blame and engaging in gossip are two manners in which leaders throw others under the bus. Another is to manipulate information and then blame others when decisions are not made with a full picture. For example, if a Principal knows that one of their staff members cannot perform certain job expectations yet places them in a position anyway, the responsibility for that decision lies with the leader. If the employee has made a good faith effort to inform their employer that they cannot walk up four flights of stairs, for example, the employee should not be put in a position to be blamed when a student safety situation arises on the fourth floor.

In the situation above, the employee has not been put in a position to be successful. Compromising student safety to blame an employee for their physical shortcomings is poor leadership. In some cases, the Principal may feel like they are building a case to get rid of an employee. This is also poor leadership. Coaching and exit plans can be put into place in a manner that preserves the employee's dignity—and they should be.

Some environments are rife with politics and getting thrown under the bus may be a common occurrence. If that is the case, it is even more admirable to rise above this strife and accept responsibility when things go wrong. These environments are not pleasant working cultures and colleagues know that. It takes courage to break the cycle of throwing others under the bus.

There are strategies to employ to help break this cycle and develop more positive leadership habits around blame. Building trusting relationships and soliciting input for decisions is among the most important. Leaders often throw others under the bus when they believe that decisions are about "them." They are not. Decisions are about students and the school community. Rarely will any individual possess all the necessary knowledge to make decisions. Empowering others to give their input is a key first step.

Once input is solicited, however, there may be a point in time where a decision has to be made. This step falls to the leader, by formal position, legal authority, payroll status, and other indicators. The leader is the one that has to ultimately land the plane. Communicating the "why" behind a decision after soliciting input is strategic. With any decision, large or small, there will always be some people that disagree. That should be expected and is okay. Communicating "why" the decision landed a particular way at least provides the rationale and provides the leader the opportunity to publicize the feedback they solicited.

Finally, building trust entails recognizing the good work that is happening throughout the organization. Recognizing others' success is a key ingredient to culture change. Publicly praising staff, celebrating successes, and intentionally thanking team members can go a long way towards developing a new culture of praise rather than one of blame. This surfaces good work happening throughout an organization and builds trust with all stakeholders.

One additional area to address deals with supervisors. A cardinal rule should be that employees never throw their supervisor under the bus. Inevitably, the supervisor will find out. Having face to face conversations about disagreements is far better than gossiping behind a supervisor's back or blaming them for one's own shortcomings. Not only does this break down trust throughout the organization, but it may also hinder chances for promotion or other opportunities. Leaders want to provide opportunities for those that they trust, and usually do not seek blame-deflectors on their teams.

This is especially true for school leaders seeking to move up either within their current organization or in another district. When applications are being reviewed and references being called, leaders tend to call other leaders to get the inside scoop on work ethic, performance, and attitude. Throwing the boss under the bus is not a career advancement strategy.

Throwing others under the bus can happen in both small and large ways. When thinking about their decisions and outcomes, leaders should ask "do I accept responsibility for the decisions made, or find others to deflect blame onto?"

Chapter 28

Failing to Focus on Continuous Improvement

Leaders fail to focus on continuous improvement when they neglect prioritization and ignore systems in their buildings and organizations. One of a leader's most important tasks is communicating what is—and is not—important. If everything is important, then nothing is important. Similarly, leaders can use this prioritization to focus on building systems that work towards continuous improvement in those high-leverage areas.

While systems-level continuous improvement is important, leaders also should focus on continually improving themselves as administrators and professionals. This personal-level focus contributes to systems-level improvement because the most important gift a leader can give their school is a better version of themselves.

Continuous improvement focused on self-leadership encompasses several areas. First, physical and mental health are priorities. The two focus areas are two sides of the same coin and slippage in one area necessarily impacts the other. On the physical side, school administrators need a certain amount of energy to be available to stakeholders. Building leaders, in particular, need to be out and about, checking in, touching base, and listening to stakeholders. Neglecting physical health limits effectiveness to carry this out.

On the mental side, leaders are bombarded with issues and concerns all day and often beyond the day. Being present and listening to each concern with empathy requires significant amounts of mental energy. While the stakeholder's concern may be the first that they brought forward in a given day, it may be the 50th concern the leader has heard that day. Giving the 50th concern the same attention as the first concern requires being in good headspace.

Neglecting sleep, healthy eating habits, and exercise can add up over time to slippage in physical and mental health. These impacts may not be noticeable on the first or second day, but over time can result in poor leadership practices. Leaders would do well to check their habits in these areas and

111

improve upon practices that fall into this category. Chances are that significant changes are not needed, but little habits like going to bed 30 minutes earlier or avoiding dessert on work nights can have significantly positive leadership effects.

Doubling down on personal health habits will have a positive impact on the building and organization. By prioritizing one's own physical and mental health, the leader not only models this for staff, but also trends towards prioritizing goals with their staff and stakeholders. Intentionality around mission, vision, and goals helps staff and stakeholders cut through the weeds and focus energies on the high-leverage activities that most impact student success.

For leaders, focusing on continuous improvement does not mean creating elaborate vision statements or engaging in heroic leadership activities. This is what separates effective leadership in the movies from effective leadership in real life. In the movies, a hero swoops in and saves the day. In fact, many aspiring and practicing school leaders erroneously hone in on this leadership style. The heroic style, however, is misleading. Because it focuses on the "hero"—the leader themselves—it misses the mark.

Real leadership towards continuous improvement is more mundane and less sexy. It is often understated and takes a "we" approach rather than a "me" approach. Imagine walking into a main office and seeing a whirlwind of activity—and not being able to tell who was "in charge." Each team member knows the system and their role within it—and how to help each other accomplish the building's goals. It matters little who answers the phone or attends to visitors in the lobby. Roles are defined but also flexible enough to respond to any given situation. Most importantly, the leader understands the value a high-functioning main office plays in building success.

Notice in the vignette above how the leader works alongside staff rather than directing orders from their likely-spacious principal's office. The leader is in the thick of things and experiencing the building's ebbs and flows first hand. They are well-positioned to experience the system and ascertain where improvements can be made. This goes beyond having an "open door policy." While that is well and good, leaders who focus on continuous improvement step outside the open door and into the organization's fast lanes. Working alongside staff—teachers, main office staff, aides, monitors, custodial— builds trust in the team and allows for the leader to experience systems and engage in conversation with those closest to them.

The aforementioned mundane leadership practices that are highlighted in the scenario above include:

- Being a "physical participant" in the work. If highlighting the building's musical program is a priority, then helping custodial teams set up and tear down will help the leader understand how this system works.

This goes beyond being "out and about" to being "actively involved" in the work.

- Asking questions and listening to feedback. If reducing playground disciplinary referrals is a priority, working alongside and asking recess monitors about their ideas towards this goal is a great step.
- Constantly communicating goals. Every meeting and every conversation is an opportunity to reinforce the priorities. This does not mean hitting people over the head constantly, but connecting conversations back to these priorities when appropriate.

Working alongside custodial teams when setting up for a musical event is not a leadership tactic likely covered in graduate school. Getting into the weeds with these activities, however, opens up several ways for leaders to improve their systems. These little practices, carried out over time and in several areas, will give even new leaders tremendous experience in crafting priorities, vision, and goals.

Focusing on personal and organizational continuous improvement does not entail significant changes in a leader's life. It may entail looking at their leadership from a different vantage point—less heroic and more mundane. Doing so will help leaders determine where priorities lie, and in working hand-in-hand with staff, build a shared sense of that vision. Leaders should ask themselves how they are focusing on continuous improvement in their personal and organizational lives, or are they at all?

Chapter 29

Delegating Up

In all organizations, especially those large and layered, delegating up can hinder collective and individual effectiveness. In layman's terms, delegating up means pushing responsibility and decision-making up one level with the intent to avoid accountability for one's actions. In essence, it lets others off the hook for problems and decisions and pushes work onto the employee's manager, who likely has their own work to complete.

Leaders need to be on the lookout for delegating up and prepared to respond if needed. Most school leaders go into administration because they want to help others and make a difference, and accepting another's delegating may be helpful at first. Especially for those with Type-A personalities, accepting others' work as their own is a slippery slope. What can begin as a helpful "second set of eyes" can devolve into full-out task takeover. This is a sure recipe for burnout and overwork.

Accepting a delegating up approach by others also permits other employees to continue with inadequate work and invites delegating up to happen again. Often, when a lower-level employee delegates up, it reveals that the employee either lacks confidence, skills, or experience to successfully perform their job functions. Rather than inviting coaching and improvement, leaders who accept this upward task flow enable employees to continue with their status quo.

Why does delegating work upward happen in the first place? All school leaders have to complete a preparation program which includes an internship experience. Then, as leaders progress through a career path, they should gain skills along the way that prepare them for increasingly-complex positions. By the time leaders achieve a principal or director position, for example, they should have acquired the necessary skill set to successfully manage their workload without burdening their supervisors.

Delegating up still occurs, however, for several reasons. First, school leaders often land in positions for which they are not fully prepared. There is on-the-job training in all positions, but some positions require more craft knowledge than others. A Committee on Special Education Chairperson position, for example, requires a detailed and specific skill set. Someone hired into that position without a special education background, for example, will need coaching and mentoring.

Moreover, delegating up may occur when a school leader finds themselves in a poor positional fit. Fit is one of the most important components for leadership effectiveness. Successful principals in one district may not find the same level of success in others. For principals in small districts where only one elementary school exists, for example, may have the freedom to make independent decisions. That same principal, now in a district with ten elementary schools, may not have the same freedom. The need to be consistent with other buildings may fly in the face of the principal's independent mindset. The fit in the latter position would not be as tight as the former.

Not all delegating up falls on the individual employee, however. School leaders who manage a large team may have difficulty staying out of the operating role. In these cases, although they may think they are helping, leaders are actually micromanaging. Team members may feel undermined and believe that the leader will make the final decision anyway, so their efforts matter little. Leaders with Type-A, detailed-oriented tendencies should be on the lookout for these patterns within their own leadership.

The real danger with delegating up as a consistent pattern is the detrimental effect it has on the leader's time. Likely, the team leader, regardless of their role—Principal, Assistant Superintendent, Superintendent, or other—has significant responsibilities of their own to manage on a day-to-day basis. Taking on another leader's burden, as well, is a surefire path to early burnout, frustration, fatigue, and an overall decrease in leadership effectiveness.

Rather than accepting this phenomenon as reality, there are steps leaders can take to help their direct reports tackle their own responsibilities. In many cases, delegating up results from new team members stepping into unfamiliar roles. When this happens, it is incumbent upon the team leader to provide the necessary coaching and support. In this instance, the team member's need for assistance does not qualify as delegating up, at least not at first. If patterns persist for many months after this, then additional intervention may be needed.

One strategy to fend off the delegating up phenomenon is to require team members to bring two possible solutions to any discussion involving a problem. Rather than solving problems for team members, this approach helps build leadership capacity across the organization. An established protocol for these conversations can help build culture and common expectations among team members.

To start the conversation, leaders can ask their team members to analyze the "why" behind the problem or situation. This type of root cause analysis helps teams avoid similar situations in the past. If the issue is that the team member has too much on their plate or lacks the professional experience to oversee the situation, rational remedies can be applied. Work loads can be discussed or professional development and coaching can take place.

After the root cause is analyzed, the brainstormed solutions can be put on the table. Ultimately, the final resolution may not be one of the two proposed solutions, but bringing these to the table gets to the solution quicker. It also places the burden for thinking the issue through front to back on the team member, who ultimately possesses responsibility for the problem. Requiring team members to propose two possible solutions at the get-go is one approach to help them move towards solving the problem rather than delegating up responsibility for the outcome.

Leaders who consistently accept tasks and responsibilities from team members are on a quick road to burnout and frustration. Teams exist for a reason, and there is a difference between being a sounding board and accepting responsibility for others' work. Team leaders should be on top of their team members' workloads and duties, but not micromanage and accept them as their own. As aforementioned, delegating up can take place by either the team member pushing work up to their leader, or by the leader stepping in too forcefully to complete tasks.

School administrators who manage teams should take inventory of work tasks and responsibilities over the course of a week. What problems are arising, and on whose plate do they belong? After this analysis, if the administrator appears to be accepting a delegating up mentality or finds themselves micromanaging, taking the steps outlined in this chapter may be a good first step towards realigning responsibilities.

Chapter 30

Misreading Reality

Any teacher who has attended Board of Education meetings or other district-wide meetings will tell you. Often, when listening to their leadership speak about district initiatives or programs, the description given by leadership does not match the realities on the ground. The leader may not be intentionally lying; rather, they do not have a grasp of the reality of how a program is actually rolling out. This mismatch between a leader's perception and the actual reality on the ground can hinder organizational progress.

Leaders fall into bad habits around misreading reality when they fail to gather first-hand information. This tends to occur more and more as leaders move up the organizational chart. Assistant Principals and Principals, for example, work side by side with teachers and are accessible enough to gather first-hand feedback. They hear directly from students, staff, and stakeholders on a daily basis and have the opportunity to gain first-hand knowledge of how initiatives and programs are progressing.

District-level leaders, especially in larger organizations, may lack that direct contact with those on the ground. These leaders may not be in buildings every day visiting classrooms and talking directly with teachers. Furthermore, they may struggle to solicit direct and honest feedback with their leadership team. Principals and Directors, in charge of programs rolling out, may be hesitant to share bad news with their supervisors.

When feedback is not forthcoming, it can be easy to fall into habits around pushing forward despite potential pitfalls. There is always more work to do than time to do it, and this can lead to feedback loops failing to provide honest and direct feedback. The result is that work continues to push forward without leaders recognizing that pivots may be necessary. Attention to these feedback loops is essential leadership work.

Bad habits around misreading reality are the result of bad habits around feedback loops. Failing to solicit honest and direct feedback from students, staff, and stakeholders leads to false interpretations. This does not mean that leaders intentionally shut off feedback. Rather, in their busy work and home lives, school leaders may fail to check in with those in their feedback loops. To tap into these feedback loops, there are specific steps leaders can take in order to hear direct and honest feedback.

First, direct and honest feedback stems from a trusting culture. Staff and stakeholders cannot be fearful of their feedback's impact on their own professional standing. In too many cultures, people clam up or simply feign consent because it is less risky than being professionally honest. In these cultures, all the feedback loops in the world will not make a difference. Staff and stakeholders must know that their leaders have only the organization's best interest in mind to facilitate these direct and honest conversations.

Additionally, intentional communication systems are necessary to support direct and honest feedback so leaders do not misread reality. These can take several forms. Regular physical presence in school buildings facilitates trust on the ground. The more staff see their leaders—especially district-level leaders—in the hallways and in classrooms, the more comfortable they will feel in providing direct and honest feedback.

Moreover, regular surveys and feedback instruments may also be helpful in garnering input. Annual surveys on professional development needs, for example, not only provide a snapshot of current realities but historical data upon which to perceive past initiatives and programs. Both current needs and changing needs over time are important feedback mechanisms in this case. With so many digital tools at the leader's disposal today, developing and implementing such feedback instruments is easier than ever.

Finally, regular ways to take the organization's temperature are important. With live, synchronous meeting capabilities, leaders can hold open office hours for staff or stakeholders to provide feedback. Regular debriefing meetings after major events, moreover, can also be a tool to garner direct and honest feedback and plan for future roll-outs. The time for these meetings is immediately after a program ends; memories are fresh and lessons learned can be garnered. Simply having these types of meetings, moreover, signals to staff that their feedback matters. The more staff feel that their direct and honest feedback is important, the more likely they are to actually provide it.

These feedback loops are both formal and informal. Regularly-scheduled meetings—both in-person and over a live, synchronous platform—are important but unstructured check-ins are as well. Leaders should look to prioritize both of these approaches when seeking to solicit direct and honest feedback about programs and initiatives.

Leaders also misread reality when they do not truly want to know what is happening on the ground. It is easier to stand up at a Board of Education meeting and sing a program's praises than it is to gather feedback on all the ways an initiative has to change and improve. Often, leaders are personally tied-up with an initiative that they themselves brought to their districts. When this happens, soliciting direct and honest feedback can be a challenge.

In reality, it is in these cases that gathering such feedback builds the most trust. When staff know that the district's overall success is more important than any hand-picked program or initiatives, and their thinking on these items matter, they will be more likely to provide this input when asked. Cynicism is less likely to build in such an environment. After all, one sign of a strong organization is the willingness to pivot when needed or even jettison a program if it is not meeting desired results.

If leaders are not receiving direct and honest feedback, they should examine their feedback loops and whether staff are comfortable providing such input. This can avoid bad habits around misreading reality and establishing a disconnect between the official district line and what is actually happening on the ground. Leaders should ask themselves, "how do they know that staff and stakeholders are comfortable providing direct and honest feedback?"

Chapter 31

Being a Bad Communicator

Communication skills have never been more important for school leaders. In today's leadership world, constant communication has become the norm. Whereas once upon a time, leaders could dictate memos for their secretaries to refine and finalize, in today's world constant emails, text messages, and other synchronous and asynchronous communication methods abound. The ability to convey a message to a wide variety of stakeholder groups has never been more important.

Communication clearly is among the most important skills a leader can possess. While this goes beyond writing to encompass speaking, body language, and other nonverbal cues, in today's world, leaders often communicate voluminously through written word. The days of formal memos have passed by and today's writing is often through less formal, but more frequent communication.

LESS FORMAL, MORE FREQUENT WRITTEN COMMUNICATION

That less formal, but more frequent communication can make or break leaders. It can be easy to slip into bad communication habits by sending hundreds of informal emails per week. Moreover, the advent of other asynchronous communication mediums such as smartphone apps, digital classroom communication boards, and other methods expands the less formal, but more frequent communication pathways. While the days of formal memos may have passed by, the current communication pathways mean that leaders are often sending more messages than their predecessors and should be aware of how those messages are being received.

The challenges with less formal, but more frequent communication pathways are many. In an email, text message, or other asynchronous pathway, welcoming greetings may feel less important. In reality, they are more important than ever. Beginning messages with enthusiastic greetings and ending them with warm salutations are important because they set the tone for message consistency. Because these more frequent messages are hitting stakeholder consciousness in larger volume than the older, more formal memos did, it is more important that they be consistently welcoming.

In addition, these messages should still maintain at least a modicum of formal syntax and style. One-sentence messages without a welcoming and ending often come across as blunt and cold. In addition, a blunt and cold message coming from a supervisor may leave stakeholders feeling that they did something wrong. Particularly in regards to email, messages should maintain similar structures to written memos. A warm welcome and strong structure lend emails an air of authenticity that can go a long way in asynchronous communication.

Text messages and other digital pathways may be more informal, but should also maintain good writing practices. Leaders should refrain from going too far down the road of completely informal practices such as emojis, substituting full words for one-letter symbols (i.e.,., writing "u" instead of "you"). Leaders should be cognizant that they are always communicating from the vantage point of being the leader. Our writing may take on more informal prose in a digital environment, but the professional symbolism of being a leader does not go away. Stakeholders will often judge messages by their professional veneer. Too many emojis, inappropriate emojis, and too-informal syntax may detract from a message's effectiveness.

When considering writing habits, leaders should ask themselves the following important questions:

- Am I intentional about starting my messages with a warm and welcoming greeting and ending them in a similar manner?
- If I were a stakeholder receiving my message, would I feel welcomed and valued?

One particularly useful practice may be for leaders to go back and read several emails sent to staff and stakeholders over the last week (an email system's Sent Items would have these saved automatically) and review messages in light of the questions above.

FACE-TO-FACE COMMUNICATION

Face-to-face communication is more frequent than ever as synchronous, live communication (i.e., Zoom, Google Meet) came into our lives during the recent pandemic. Leaders can assume that some of those mediums will remain useful even as schools return to some normalcy in the future. Therefore, many conversations that used to be phone calls may continue as live, synchronous meetings.

In a live, synchronous meeting, face to face communication skills take on more importance than during a phone call. Body language becomes more important as your fellow communicators can see you, at least from the shoulders up. The same communication habits that can hinder in-person communication can have the same impact in this environment.

Conveying enthusiasm and warmth—also known as "emotional contagion"—is especially important early in a relationship to establish trust.[1] Several studies have demonstrated the link between smiling employees and customer satisfaction and it would make sense that such theories also translate into the school leadership world. Positive emotions conveyed by smiling and enthusiasm may influence an individual's subjective judgments and interpretations. It stands safe to say, therefore, that school leaders who understand emotional contagion will develop more positive relationships with stakeholders than those who do not.

Whether live communication is face to face or over a synchronous platform, smiling is crucial to establishing emotion and tone. Messages delivered with enthusiasm and warmth are far more likely to resonate than those delivered in a colder manner. School leaders should test this theory for themselves. Try conveying extra warmth and enthusiasm for one week and reflect upon the results. Chances are that more of those messages will be met with returned enthusiasm and warmth since emotions are contagious.

For leaders, this emotional labor can be taxing and stressful. Understanding that leadership emotions are contagious also brings with it the increased stress of that realization. The more a leader practices delivering messages with warmth and enthusiasm, however, the more habit-forming it will become. Leaders who have fallen into dour communication habits would do well to start building better habits as soon as possible.

When considering face to face communication habits, leaders may ask themselves a series of questions to reflect upon their practices:

- How much do I smile when speaking with others? Consider asking someone to record a staff meeting or other function and review your body language, smiling, and other verbal and nonverbal communication practices.
- If I were on the receiving end of my messages, what emotions would I experience?
- Is there someone I work with who does this well? Could I ask them for advice?

NOTE

1. Otterbring, T. (2017). Smile for a while: the effect of employee-displayed smiling on customer affect and satisfaction. Journal of Service Management, 28(2): 284–304. https://doi.org/10.1108/JOSM-11-2015-0372.

Chapter 32

Lack of Patience with Outcomes

Ask any veteran teacher about curriculum initiates over their career and you are likely to hear a common theme: every couple of years, a new program was implemented requiring professional learning, data analysis, and valuable onboarding time. Then, after the program failed to produce immediate results, it was scrapped for another program. This cycle of program after program ultimately stems from a lack of patience with outcomes.

Overnight success is usually a myth. Every now and again, the stars align and school improvement happens like it does in the movies. A new leader enters the scene, inspires all staff and students, and everything falls into place seamlessly. In all reality, school improvement does not operate that way at all. It takes time to build relationships, onboard programs, and make incremental improvements.

Continually switching and swapping programs, moreover, leads to cynicism and burnout among school staff. Schools can take on any improvement program, but they cannot take on *every* improvement program. New leaders entering a school or organization are better suited to listen to what has been working and build upon it initially rather than promote different programs or initiatives. Particularly among veteran staff, leaders should honor the experiences and listen for what works and what does not work rather than force an outside vision upon a school or organization.

While qualitative outcomes are inherent in school improvement, quantitative measures are often what drives the process. Data points such as test scores, reading levels attainment, attendance rates, and other hard numbers do not tell the entire story, but they do indicate areas of strength and those needing more attention. Rather than eschewing the data as meaningless, effective leaders learn to harness incremental improvements to build momentum for ongoing programs and initiatives.

Research has demonstrated that small wins maintain focus for school improvement's long-term goals. By focusing on incremental progress, leaders can maintain positive motion towards school improvement. Furthermore, by communicating short-term successes as stepping stones towards long-term school improvement, staff are able to see how small wins contribute to the overall picture. Short-term progress reinforces goal persistence and maintains focus on longer-term, bigger-picture outcomes.[1]

Moreover, building leaders may be under pressure from their central office to show immediate improvement. Advocating for building staff while meeting the central office's expectations is one of the true challenges for building leaders. To stave off the continual churn in programs and initiatives, building leaders can take specific steps to publicize their short-term wins for staff and stakeholders. Making these results "noisy" reinforces short-term progress and continues to build momentum towards long-term goals.

For example, if a building has a goal to reduce chronic absenteeism by 15% over the course of two school years, leaders can take initial steps to ensure short-term wins. Identifying the most chronically absent students, checking in every morning, making positive phone calls, and other small steps may lead to several students improving their attendance. Keeping that data biweekly to demonstrate progress is important. Rather than wait until the end of the marking period or quarter to publicize results, breaking down goal attainment into smaller chunks is important.

Once goals are broken into small chunks, making them visible for all to see is critical. Bulletin boards demonstrating progress, in conspicuous areas of the school, is one way to publicize these results. Posting daily rates of attendance and looking for trends helps build goal persistence among staff and publicizes results for all staff to see. Part of building momentum is onboarding all staff—not only teachers but support staff, as well. Once a goal starts building momentum, it is likely that more and more staff will buy-in and want to jump on board towards contributing to the improvement.

Gaining buy-in and commitment for any initiative is challenging work. Most staff have seen leaders and programs come and go, and often think "this too shall pass." To gain trust and successfully onboard a new program takes time. Once that buy-in is earned, leaders need to be patient with outcomes. Not all programs work, of course; jettisoning a program is not necessarily a sign of failure. Rather, it could be determined that the program is not a good fit once implementation begins. Those decisions, however, should be made collaboratively with the same teams that initially developed buy-in. Leaders should not offload programs unilaterally due to a lack of patience with outcomes.

Leaders who lack patience with outcomes are often those who have developed some of the following small, yet detrimental, habits:

- Attending conferences and returning with new books to engage staff in building-wide book studies.

- Pushing too many change initiatives at once; rather than overload staff, leaders should work collaboratively with staff to generate buy-in and commitment around only a few "high-leverage" ideas. These would be ideas that, if implemented well, would result in school improvement across several areas.
- Going for short-term wins to boost one's own resume for future promotions; staff can sniff this out a mile away.

Publicizing short-term wins in pursuit of long-term goals will help develop commitment and momentum around a strategically-chosen set of programs. In addition, building off of successful programs already in place can help staff connect the dots for any future change initiatives. While leaders can pivot within long-term goals if facets need reconsideration, they should be realistic that real change takes time. Before onboarding any new program or initiative, leaders should ask themselves "am I willing to invest multiple years to see this initiative through in working collaboratively with staff?"

NOTE

1. Kaitlin Wooley & Ayelet Fishbach. *Immediate rewards predict adherence to long-term goals.* Personality and Social Psychology Bulletin, 2017. Volume 43, No. 2, 151–162. DOI: 10.1177/0146167216676480.

Chapter 33

Rating Employees with One's Own Personal Measuring Stick

Teachers, counselors, social workers, and other professionals enter into school leadership for a number of reasons. For some, working for an ineffective leader is motivation for trying to improve the system. For others, dedication to helping students is so strong that they want to bring their influence to another level. In most cases, aspiring and practicing school leaders are willing to dedicate more hours than the average employee to pursuing their leadership degree and securing their first position.

These are all legitimate reasons for entering into school leadership, especially the desire to put in the extra time to improve outcomes for students. Once securing into school leadership, however, there is a danger in expecting all employees to share in these goals. Rating employees by one's own personal measuring stick is a dangerous habit for leaders to fall into. Leaders should have high standards for their staff and hold them accountable for their work. The danger, however, is expecting every single employee to share a 24/7/365 passion and dedication to their jobs that leaders may hold.

Assuming a leadership position necessitates more time, more commitment, and more involvement than remaining a teacher or similar position. Recognizing and accepting that trade-off is important. Being at the concert, attending school events, being accessible after work hours and on weekends, and having the school on one's mind all of the time are emblematic of all effective school leaders. Those who are not in leadership positions do not have to carry that burden. Expecting them to do so is a sure way to alienate staff and break down trust.

Much research exists on effective school leadership's impact on staff morale, school culture, and student outcomes. Instructional leadership, transformational leadership, and other positive, research-based paradigms have been studied and validated as impactful for schools, cultures, and students. Research also exists, however, on bad leadership's negative impact. Some studies have indicated that bad leadership is actually more impactful than good leadership, albeit in the opposite direction.[1] Leader-member exchange theory posits that the quality of interactions between a supervisor and an employee impacts the organization in several ways. The more positive and resource-driven this interaction becomes, the more the employee will be willing to engage with the organization's goals.[2] Therefore, leaders should pay close attention to how they are explicitly and implicitly rating employees as their actions and inactions will have consequences for employee morale.

Often, leaders communicate their expectations to staff in ways they may not realize. These interactions may include:

- Sending emails to staff on off-hours. While a leader may reasonably believe that they can read their email whenever they wish and not feel compelled to respond, employees often react differently when receiving communication from their supervisor. Simply receiving an email from a boss can trigger employees to start thinking about work on their off-hours.
- Waiting outside an employee's door for a conversation immediately after their class ends. Most employees need some time to gather materials— or themselves. Being an immediate presence to discuss an issue at that time communicates to staff that they, too, should be continually thinking about the same things as the leader.
- Expressing frustration when an employee drops the ball on a project. Everyone comes to their positions with different challenges and complexities, and no one is perfect. Providing support rather than expressing frustration is important.

Comparing employees to oneself is one negative leadership habit; comparing employees to each other is another. Comparing one employee to another is like comparing one child to another; rather than motivate, the comparison acts to divide. The fact is that no one person experiences things quite like anyone else. While some staff are motivated by extrinsic rewards, others are driven by internal satisfaction. Comparing employees to one another misses the mark for leaders who are seeking to build trusting relationships.

Comparing employees to oneself and to others negatively impacts leadership effectiveness. On the other hand, helping employees grow by having reflective conversations, one-on-one coaching meetings, and other collaborative experiences may be a better measurement tool. In public education, management rights are often limited in terms of reassigning or moving staff. In many ways, this is a positive. Rather than being able to rid themselves of what they perceive as ineffective employees, leaders must find ways to build relationships with staff. In the long run, this is a much more effective way to lead than to rely on extrinsic carrots and sticks.

Involving employees in measuring themselves necessitates building trusting relationships with all staff, regardless of position. Valuing and affirming support staff, in particular, is key. Leaders can implement several steps to begin this journey, including:

- Putting into place a strong onboarding program for new hires. While teachers usually progress through a professional program and new teacher orientation sessions, support staff are often hired one day and start the next. Some support staff may never have worked in schools or directly with children. Helping these new hires learn best practices right away helps to build trusting relationships and demonstrates value.
- Engage in quarterly reflections with not only new hires, but all staff. While this may not be mandated in a contract, a strong reflective practice—either formally through a written protocol or informally through conversation—helps to collaboratively discuss strengths and areas for growth.
- Implementing, in all year end evaluations, areas for growth. These should be identified by the employee. Even the best employees have areas in which they can grow. Building a growth ethic within a school builds momentum towards employees measuring themselves against their own self-identified goals.

When considering their evaluative methods and metrics, leaders should ask themselves "am I expecting my staff to be like me, or like others, or become better versions of themselves?

NOTES

1. Baumeister, R. F., Bratslavsky, E., Finkenauer, C., & Vohs, K. D. (2001). Bad is stronger than good. *Review of General Psychology, 5*, 323–370. https://doi.org/10.1037//1089-2680.5.4.323.

2. Lee, J. (2005). Effects of leadership and leader-member exchange on commitment. *Leadership & Organization Development Journal, 26*, 655–672. https://doi.org/10.1108/01437730510633728.

Chapter 34

Seeking Comfort over Discomfort

Many educational leaders are familiar with Malcolm Gladwell's claim in *Outliers* that any skill requires 10,000 practice hours to demonstrate mastery. That statement, based on a 1993 research study into deliberate practice, states that skill and performance differences among even elite performers is less about innate talent and more about effortful practice.[1] Getting better at anything, according to this theory, is more about getting outside of one's comfort zone than it is being innately gifted or skilled.

This lesson is insightful for school leaders who are either launching their administrative career in their first position or taking on new responsibilities. Effective leaders often seem like they "have it all" and effortlessly tackle issue after issue with success. These leaders, from the outside looking in, easily build strong relationships and their schools possess strong cultures and positive outcomes. Below the surface, however, it is likely that these leaders intentionally sought out discomfort over their careers. By seeking discomfort over comfort, they continually expanded their comfort zone and engaged in thousands of hours of deliberate practice.

Because it is hard to see on the surface, it is easy to miss the success lessons these leaders demonstrate. Seeking discomfort over comfort does not mean that leaders should take reckless chances and engage in risky behavior. It does not, for example, mean that leaders should ignore their training and go against the grain in ways that compromises their leadership. It does, however, mean that leaders should seek out opportunities to expand their comfort zone in safe, repeatable ways that build up their leadership capacity over time.

Increasing one's comfort zone should initially begin with caution. Positive experiences in stepping outside of one's comfort zone will lead to additional endeavors in that direction. For building leaders who seek to gain experience in a curricular area in which they are not familiar, participating in professional learning alongside teachers is a positive first step. Seeking discomfort does not mean that the leader has to suddenly be the expert in such an area.

They can be vulnerable, learn alongside expert teachers, and build a collaborative relationship around moving the initiative forward.

This is an example of a safe first step. By attending an initial professional learning session, the leader will expand their knowledge base and learn additional ways to support their teachers. This will, in turn, lead to future learning opportunities to see the program in practice in the classroom and offer substantive feedback. Over time, safe forays into new learning areas will build a knowledge base that allows leaders to support their teachers in a number of programs and initiatives.

Moreover, expanding a comfort zone is often successful when the deliberate practice can be repeated over time. For leaders who are uncomfortable with difficult parent conversations, engaging families in a proactive manner can yield benefits. By talking with families often, leaders can avoid their initial interactions being around challenging topics. Deliberating calling families on a regular basis and communicating through other mediums builds a comfort level with this practice. Over time, families come to trust leaders who consistently communicate, especially around positive interactions.

Not all discomfort may be around safe and repeatable activities, of course. There are numerous leadership responsibilities that are uncomfortable regardless of the context. For example, a personnel director may be uncomfortable calling unsuccessful teacher candidates to let them know they did not receive the job. Being the bearer of bad news is never comfortable, even for seasoned leaders. In this case, however, informing interviewed candidates of the process's conclusion—especially when they are not the successful candidate—is a positive practice.

While every now and again someone may become personally upset with the caller, most candidates appreciate the closure such a call brings to the process. In addition, it puts the organization in a positive light that they had enough respect to inform unsuccessful candidates that they did not earn the position. If necessary, leaders can develop a script for such calls and practice that script over time. Even in these uncomfortable practices that may never become fully comfortable, keeping the other person's respect in mind can help alleviate stress.

Nobody has the market cornered on seeking discomfort over comfort. Finding safe avenues, engaging in deliberate practice, and finding the benefit even when the task remains challenging are all important. Self-doubt, however, is part of the process. Even the most successful, outward-facing leaders have had to face down their self-doubt and persevere through discomfort. Most likely, successful leaders have found success because they did push through such times.

Seeking mentors to help navigate these challenges is important for leaders. Often, this should be someone outside of one's immediate organization since some issues may involve office politics or intraorganizational concerns. Every move within school leadership—from teacher to administrator, from assistant principal to principal, from building level to district level—includes different stressors. Successful principals, for example, may find that the issues they deal with at the district level are different in nature than at the building level. Often, they are more complex as they involve several buildings at once.

Therefore, it is important for leaders to intentionally seek out mentors that can assist them in navigating activities that expand their comfort zone. Chances are, others have had to handle similar issues in the past. Learning from other's experiences not only builds capacity but also helps leaders realize that they are not alone. Stepping outside of one's comfort zone and realizing that it will be okay in the end is powerful. Mentors can help leaders safely navigate that process.

NOTE

1. Ericsson, K. A., Krampe, R. T., & Tesch-Römer, C. (1993). The Role of Deliberate Practice in the Acquisition of Expert Performance. *Psychological Review, 100*(3), 363–406. https://doi.org/10.1037/0033-295X.100.3.363.

Chapter 35

Tolerating Subpar Performance

Employee management is one of a leader's most important tasks. Solid hiring practices, free from implicit bias, and a good onboarding program are also key components. Once employees are on board, however, it is critical for leaders to continually offer feedback and support to their staff. Too often, however, leaders end up tolerating subpar performance because it does not rise to crisis levels.

Some employee behavior is easy to recognize and either support or ameliorate. High performers stand out for their consistent excellence and poor performers are flagged due to lack of observable traits such as punctuality, timeliness, or follow-through, or less visible characteristics, such as needing support for classroom management on a daily basis. It is often those subpar, but not poor, performers that are overlooked. These employees tend to hang onto positions at greater rates than completely poor performers and have a far more detrimental impact on building culture and student achievement.

High performers are publicly recognized and poor performers should be coached out of their roles, but subpar performers often do just enough to remain in their positions. They tend to "hang onto" their positions for a potential number of reasons:

- Leaders "like" them and develop appropriate, yet personal relationships with them. They may be nice human beings, but not very good employees.
- Their performance is "not quite" as bad as others; by comparison, they are not the worst employees in the building and can get by being below average because they are not downright terrible.
- Their behavior and poor performance is chalked up to "just the way they are." Some staff just "cannot get along with some students," so it goes. Because an employee has been this way for so long, any support or difficult conversation is viewed as futile.

In addition, leaders tolerate subpar performance because the benefits of addressing the issue are not immediately evident. The subpar employee may have relationships in the building and any difficult conversation could have the potential to impact other staff. Moreover, colleagues may not be voicing their displeasure with the subpar performer with leadership. There may be whisperings about how people really feel, but those feelings are not out in the open. Leaders may feel that addressing a subpar employee could negatively impact building morale since it appears that few others are bothered by the performance.

In reality, the opposite is true. If the leader is noticing subpar performance, then colleagues—who spend more time around each other than does the leader—are assuredly also taking note. Most employees will not want to "be the one" to cause conflict among colleagues and will resort to talking about subpar performance in the staff room or venting about it to others. Therefore, it is up to leaders to have their ear to the ground and be attuned to how staff are feeling about such issues.

Addressing subpar performance does not need to be conflict-ridden. Certainly, some employees will take offense to their subpar performance being surfaced and discussed. Most employees will rationalize their behavior in any number of ways—they are late because the drive to work is longer than others, they always seem to have the "bad kids" in class, or other excuses. Leaders should anticipate this. Very rarely will employees come into the leader's office and admit that their performance is not up to par, or that improvements need to be made. At the end of the day, leaders should refrain from "owning" this reaction. The employee's reaction is far more about the employee than it is about the leader who is doing their job in surfacing underperformance.

Anticipating these reactions, there are specific steps that leaders can take to help subpar employees improve their performance. Step one should be coaching and supporting. First, the difference between events and trends should be noted. An employee who is late one or two tim3es is different from one who is consistently late. Everyone has events in their life that crop up; it is quite different when trends are noted.

If trends are noted, leaders should begin informally documenting on their own. Having objective evidence for the initial conversation is critical. Many employees will become defensive and may feel they are being singled out. Having data—dates and times, direct observations, frequency—makes the conversation less about feelings and more about facts. The first step is coaching and supporting the employees, while grounding the conversation in as many objective facts as possible.

After the trends are noted, the subpar performance should be connected to the overall school environment. A school monitor who is ten minutes late every day, for example, compromises the safety of students and also places an undue burden on their fellow monitors who have to pick up the slack. A main office staff member who greets parents less-than-warmly at the front desk harms the overall impression that families have of the school. Connecting these trends to the overall school—depersonalizing them in essence—hopefully helps the employee see their actions in the overall context.

From here, several pathways are possible. Ideally, the employee recognizes, to the greatest degree possible, that improvement needs to be made. Leaders should offer support and encouragement. The employee should know that they are valued, and that improvement in this area will bolster the overall school climate and culture. The goal is for all staff to be positive contributors to school improvement. Depending on the issue's severity or how often coaching conversations are taking place, a written memo may also be issued. If this step is taken, it is advised that leaders work with their district personnel office.

However, not all employees will want to improve or have the capacity to improve. In these cases, coaching the staff member out of the school employment realm may be best. The employment picture should be a win-win proposition. It should be rewarding for the school and also fulfilling for the employee. When this fails to take place, the best course of action may be for the employee to seek work elsewhere. Leaders should remain supportive at all times, and offer to do whatever they can to help. Maintaining the employee's value and dignity is the goal, even when the staff member may be angry with the leader and turn negative themselves.

Regardless of the outcome, addressing subpar performance will have a positive impact on other staff members. Even though the leader-employee conversations are confidential, chances are the rest of the staff will recognize that the behavior is being addressed in some way. This is far better than not addressing it at all. True, the employee being addressed may have a friend or two on staff who back them. But the majority of employees want—and need—their colleagues to be good at their work. Holding subpar performers accountable will send positive ripples throughout the building or organization.

Tolerating subpar performance is one of the most negative leadership habits to possess because it slowly whittles away at any positive cultural gains. When leaders address this behavior, it may be uncomfortable at first, but will ultimately demonstrate to staff that everyone's job performance has value and impacts the entire team. Leaders fail to address subpar performance because it is uncomfortable and they fear that the staff member in question may become upset or angry with them. They might. Holding team members accountable is part of the leader's job; furthermore, a subpar performer's anger with the leader is well worth the cultural gains that come with addressing such behavior.

Leaders should ask themselves if they are tolerating subpar performance, and the reasons for it. Are they afraid of the negative repercussions from an angry employee?

Chapter 36

Focusing on How Things "Should Be" Rather Than How They Actually Are

While related to this book's chapter on "Misreading Reality," this small leadership habit goes beyond a failure to account for feedback loops. All leaders have an ideal state in their minds for how their schools and organizations "should be." Programs should lead directly to increased student achievement, all staff should follow all of the rules all of the time, and all stakeholders should buy into the district's mission, vision, and goals.

It is important for leaders to keep ideal states in mind. They serve a useful purpose in maintaining a vision for ultimate outcomes while persisting towards those goals. Leaders may fall into bad habits, however, when they conflate progress towards that ideal state with the ideal state itself. In reality, the ideal state will never truly be achieved. Schooling's very nature makes this the case.

Because schooling is human dependent—meaning, it is about people—conditions are dynamic and often change. Progress cannot be linear because human beings are not linear. This does not mean that progress cannot be made; rather, it means that leaders should be careful how they measure progress towards this ideal state. Furthermore, leaders who are frustrated by lack of progress or its dynamic nature expend valuable energy focused on the wrong thing.

Chances are, "how things actually are" is probably representative of progress made. In some cases, schools and organizations have to start from rock bottom and work their way back up. But in most cases, schools already possess high levels of expertise, experience, and past success in some areas. While it is likely not the ideal state, "how things actually are" may represent significant strengths and progress.

Building upon strengths is a means towards an end. It validates staff efforts and recognizes, even if outcomes are not perfect, they reflect good work being completed. For leaders, their reality is that they no longer teach kids. Therefore, leaders have to work through staff to reach the students. Validating the expertise and experience that already exists is a powerful way to start building towards an ideal state.

Additionally, leaders waste significant energy when they become frustrated by the way things "should be." In any organization, a continuum of staff needs are inevitable. Without leadership, initiatives and programs tend to drift off course. If a program drifts a little off course for five years in a row, course corrections will be needed to bring it back on track. Part of allowing for this drift occurs when leaders try to force an ideal state onto a dynamic and ever-changing environment.

Avenues to distract leaders from "the way things actually are" exist throughout the profession. Leaders may follow other leaders on social media and compare their building's outcomes to their neighbors. They may see a social media post about another school district's back to school night and see hundreds of parents in attendance while their own similar event drew hardly a few. In these situations, it is easy to perceive someone else possessing this ideal state and falling into a comparison trap.

Letting go of these comparison traps is essential for seeing things the way they actually are. Every school and district is different. There are different communities, school sizes, configurations, and budgetary realities. While this is not an excuse to push forward towards an ideal state, it is a reminder that everyone is somewhere on the journey. Leaders cannot know the specifics behind these broadcast events, or the reality behind these social media posts. It is just as likely that another leader framed the event just the right way to demonstrate maximum positivity.

This may be difficult to do because most leader's identity is inherently tied up in their work. Especially true for building-level leaders and Principals in particular, language such as "my building" connotes a strong sense of identity between the personal and the professional. Personal leadership can often feel at stake when these dynamics occur. When test scores are not as high as others, for example, many leaders will take that personally and compare their outcomes to those of other schools.

Self-applied pressure, to a certain degree, is important for leaders to maintain. Leaders should feel that pressure to continually improve their schools in all ways, and seeing others' success as instructive can be useful towards that goal. When this comparison becomes toxic, however, and detracts from leadership effectiveness is when it becomes a problem. Leaders should self-monitor their emotions to determine where they are landing in this area.

When viewing someone else's social media and seeing their success, leaders can react in a number of ways that can be guideposts towards finding out where they land on this. If the immediate reaction is "wow, I could really learn from this person," the movement is towards learning and continuous growth. If the reaction, however, is "wow, their school gets that many families at parent night? Their community must care," the reaction falls into the comparison trap. "How things actually are" is likely much better than their emotions are telling them. Reaching out to learn from others is much more powerful than wallowing in self-pity.

Effective leadership comes in all shapes, sizes, and forms. For one school, a 75% passage rate on an exam may be a great accomplishment. For others, it falls short of the mark. Focusing on progress and validating the progress that has been made begets more progress. Modeling this type of thinking, moreover, helps staff view their colleagues as collaborators rather than competitors. There are many ways to be a strong leader and outcomes can look different and still represent progress towards that ideal state.

When leaders focus on the way things "should be" rather than how they "actually are," they shortchange their leadership effectiveness. Things will never truly be as they "should be" and leaders waste energy when they approach issues from that perspective. If leaders find themselves focusing on this ideal state too often, they should ask "what strengths exist right here in this school, and how can we validate and build upon them?"

Chapter 37

Overthinking How to Move Forward

Leaders have to make dozens, if not hundreds, of decisions each day, big and small. For the bigger decisions and initiatives requiring implementation, it may be easy for leaders to fall into an analysis trap. An analysis trap occurs when leaders seek out every possible angle before making decisions or moving forward.

Typically, the bigger the issues and the more people involved, the more options will be available for moving forward. On the surface, this may appear as a positive dynamic. The more options available makes it more likely that the right solution will appear. As the leader, staff are likely looking for the "right" answer to be selected so the issue can move forward. Chances are, however, that there are several "right" answers that could be applied.

Having too many options is part of the problem. There are hundreds of ways, for example, to address student attendance problems. From family engagement nights to outreach programs to automated phone calls, finding the one single best approach feels overwhelming. It should be that way, because it is. There is usually never "one" single best way to approach a large-scale issue such as chronic absenteeism or dozens of other problems.

While having broad input or committees can also lead to consensus, it may also lead to having too many options or too many opinions. Research exists to support nearly every half-way decent idea and simple Google searches can reinforce anyone's opinions that such-and-such an approach will yield the best results. In short, it is incredibly easy for leaders to fall into an analysis trap when trying to tackle meaty issues.

Sometimes, a lack of experience also contributes to overthinking. Early-career school leaders have not had the same body of work as those with several years. Learning from past initiatives and programs is a benefit that veteran leaders possess. For those early in their leadership careers, that hindsight is not yet present.

For leaders who tend to get trapped in overanalysis, precious days and weeks can go by without beginning any implementation. Going back to our attendance example, waiting an extra week or month to try something out wastes school days where students continue to exhibit concerning patterns. Getting into solutions quickly not only cuts through the analysis trap, but also cuts to the chase and begins helping students.

Finally, many school leaders pride themselves on taking an academic approach to their work. Being grounded in the research and examining an issue from all angles has its positives. When a bias to action is needed, however, being *too* academic on an issue may lead to overthinking how to move forward when just getting started on a solution is the most important step.

Rather than waiting for the master plan to develop, the best move leaders can make is to get started and measure success. For student attendance, one simple way to get started would be to identify the top-20 most absent students and make one positive phone call a day to that student's home when they are in school. For many families, school has not been a positive experience, and beginning to change that mindset can pay immediate dividends.

Would this approach move the needle towards improving attendance? The only way to find out is to implement an approach and measure its result. If results begin to improve for those twenty students, the program could be expanded to another student group. If not, then one of the most important leadership traits to avoid overthinking comes into play: the pivot.

Pivoting towards a different approach when addressing an issue is important. If a given amount of time has passed and the program has not yielded expected results, revisiting the approach is essential. Sometimes this means small tweaks could be necessary, and other times a wholesale change is needed. Successful organizations not only have a bias to action, but also are not afraid to jettison an unsuccessful approach if it does not yield results.

Being able to pivot rests on having clear outcomes. Having clear outcomes necessitates separating fact from fiction. Too often, school staff assume that their "hunches" about the data are accurate. Sometimes the data reinforces these hunches, but in other cases the data presents a different reality. Getting clear about separating fact from fiction and creating clear outcomes is essential.

For this attendance example, the outcome may be a 10% increase in average daily attendance for this student group over a six-week period. Implementing a program and tracking its progress towards that goal helps leaders determine if and when a pivot is necessary.

Too often, leaders believe that having to pivot or admit an initiative was not wholly successful is a sign of failure. In reality, the opposite is true. There are so many factors impacting school success that no one program or initiative meets with complete success. Usually, lessons can be learned from these attempts that strengthen the overall approach or point towards a different one. Rather than viewing this as a failure, it should be viewed as one more step towards success. One step at a time is realistic; having the perfect, on-the-spot solution rarely occurs.

Building this mindset across the building or organization will help promote agility among decision-makers. When students, staff, and stakeholders feel comfortable trying something, evaluating success, and pivoting when needed, they feel less pressure towards having a perfect answer. A perfect answer does not exist. When leaders model this mindset, they build this into their culture across their buildings and organization.

Overcoming overthinking, therefore, requires a bias towards action and the willingness to pivot when necessary. Often, the most challenging aspect to overcome is the leader's ego. Admitting that a certain program did not work as intended and changes need to be made can be difficult for leaders. They understand that things are not going in the right direction, but they can be hesitant to admit changes are needed.

Leaders should reflect upon a recent change initiative that did meet intended success. Did the initiative take too long to get off the ground due to overthinking? If there was an opportunity to pivot, why was it not acted upon? Getting below the surface on these questions will make it more likely that quick action and pivots occur in the future.

Chapter 38

Confusing Others' Interest with Your Own

School leaders often take personal and professional ownership of their work and their work locations. Building principals, for example, speak of "my building" or "my students" when discussing their job with others. Taking this personal and professional ownership is usually healthy and a sign of strong leadership.

Taking leadership personally and assuming personal responsibility for outcomes is important to ensure positive results. The challenge for leaders, however, is not assuming that each staff member implicitly shares those same interests. This does not mean that staff members across the board are not passionate about helping students or performing their jobs at high levels. Rather, it means that leaders should recognize that different groups may view different agendas from different vantage points.

Educating other people's children is deeply personal work. School staff bring their entire selves and lives to their jobs on a daily basis. Often, school staff are dealing with challenges outside of work that may naturally spill over into their work lives. It is important for school leaders to realize that staff are people first, and employees second. Like all people, staff bring a myriad of personal challenges, vantage points, and histories to their work.

When school leaders confuse others' interests with their own, they often are blind to these dynamics. They may be asking staff to take on challenges and responsibilities for which they are ill-equipped or unable to carry out due to outside factors. Some examples of these dynamics include:

- Pursuing an after-school program for students without taking into account that some staff have to leave school at their earliest opportunity to pick up their young children from their own schools.

- Developing lunch and recess protocols without considering the staffing capacity of those employees assigned to supervision during those unstructured times.
- Assigning additional data tracking paperwork to teachers without analyzing whether such additional responsibilities would impact teacher preparation periods.

The above scenarios all include situations where leaders have to consider multiple vantage points before implementing procedures and protocols. Building-wide goals and initiatives are important, but they often have to be implemented within the context of staffing capacity. In addition, there may be contractual considerations to take into account when assigning responsibilities to staff.

In scenarios like those above, leaders may receive questions about staff capacity or the time that such interventions would take. Too often, leaders view this as "pushback" and through a negative lens. Leaders may feel like staff are attacking their initiatives rather than asking good questions about capacity and time.

This is where leaders have to realize that each staff member has different, and competing, interests in their personal and professional lives. For teachers who need to leave with the buses to pick up their own young children, it is not that they do not want to help kids, but that they have a competing interest that needs to be met. For staff who seek to protect their preparation periods—which are often contractually required—it is not that they devalue the data collection process, but that they need that set-aside 45-minutes to prepare for the next day to do their jobs well.

Reframing "pushback" through this lens of competing personal and professional interests will help leaders understand this feedback. Realizing that staff want to help children learn as much as the leader does, but may have competing interests that intersect with initiatives, is crucial. When leaders approach these situations with this lens, they are much less likely to become negative and take such feedback personally.

It is important, therefore, to know staff members and what their competing interests may be. It is critical for leaders to get to know staff on a personal level. This does not mean going out and sharing a drink on a Friday evening; rather, the goal is to understand each staff member's personal and professional interests.

Understanding these interests can help inform building and organizational initiatives and also help leaders reframe feedback they may receive to such programs. Being attuned to these interests often includes:

- Understanding staff member's home situations and how they impact their professional lives. For example, if many staff members have young children of their own, leaders should realize that many staff members will have to leave work as soon as they are able.
- Understanding the school year's ebbs and flows. Some parts of the year are more challenging than others. For example, during state testing season, leaders may want to avoid any new initiatives until staff have the bandwidth to proceed in the direction.
- Recognizing the staff's level of experience. A more veteran staff may possess experiences that can inform such programs due to their time in the building, which is often longer than the leader's. A younger, greener staff may need more assistance framing such programs.

When leaders are cognizant of these dynamics, they are much more likely to take personal and professional interests into account and take feedback much less personally. Moreover, what some leaders may perceive as "pushback" is actually an opportunity to refine ideas further and promote their longer-term success. Staff members have vantage points that leaders do not. They may be embedded in the community or have worked in the building for many years. Rather than push that feedback to the side, leaders should pursue it.

It is important, therefore, for leaders to recognize that different staff come to work with different interests, both professional and personally. Often, these interests are somewhat different from the leader's. When pursuing programs or initiatives, leaders should keep this in mind. If they begin to receive messages that indicate something is askew, leaders should ask themselves "is this program bumping up against staff's personal or professional interests in a way they're not aware of?"7

About the Author

Larry Dake is a district-level administrator in upstate New York who, over the last dozen years, has served as a curriculum coordinator, building principal, and assistant superintendent. Prior to that, he was a high school social studies teacher. Additionally, he has taught in the Binghamton University Educational Leadership program since 2017.

Dr. Dake's first book, *Crisis Management: Effective School Leadership to Avoid Early Burnout* was published in December 2020 from Rowman & Littlefield. He has also contributed to several journals and other works on leadership practices and theories.

Dr. Dake lives in Endwell, New York, with his wife, Kelly, an elementary reading teacher, and three children ages 12, 10, and 7.

CPSIA information can be obtained
at www.ICGtesting.com
Printed in the USA
LVHW041022140323
741584LV00001B/62